ALL OVER THE COUNTRY!

"Playwright Mart Crowley has managed to cover an amazing amount of ground. . . . His dialogue is not only authentic but funny, and you don't have to be a homosexual to enjoy it. . . . a frame for emotional truth."

Life Magazine

"Convention is being exploded in THE BOYS IN THE BAND, a very funny play that takes place at an undisguisedly homosexual party. The humor is often viciously cruel and we are occasionally surprised to find ourselves laughing at remarks that we would find horrifying if made in a real-life gathering. But laugh we do."

Saturday Review

(Please turn page)

TO FIND OUT
WHAT ALL THE TALK IS ABOUT,
WE INVITE YOU TO
LOOK INSIDE AND MEET—

THE BOYS
IN
THE BAND

THE BOYS
IN
THE BAND

❧

Mart Crowley

A DELL BOOK

Published by
DELL PUBLISHING CO., INC.
750 Third Avenue
New York, N.Y. 10017

Reprinted by arrangement with
Farrar, Straus & Giroux, Inc.
New York, N.Y.

Printed in the U.S.A.
First Dell printing—June 1969

FOR
HOWARD JEFFREY
AND
DOUGLAS MURRAY

THE BOYS
IN
THE BAND

The Boys in the Band was first performed in January 1968 at the Playwrights Unit, Vandam Theatre, Charles Gnys, managing director.

The Boys in the Band was first produced on the New York stage by Richard Barr and Charles Woodward, Jr., at Theatre Four on April 14, 1968. The play was designed by Peter Harvey and directed by Robert Moore.

The original cast was:

MICHAEL	*Kenneth Nelson*
DONALD	*Frederick Combs*
EMORY	*Cliff Gorman*
LARRY	*Keith Prentice*
HANK	*Laurence Luckinbill*
BERNARD	*Reuben Greene*
COWBOY	*Robert La Tourneaux*
HAROLD	*Leonard Frey*
ALAN	*Peter White*

Characters

MICHAEL   Thirty, average face, smartly
          groomed
DONALD   Twenty-eight, medium blond,
          wholesome American
          good looks
EMORY   Thirty-three, small, frail, very
          plain
LARRY   Twenty-nine, extremely
          handsome
HANK   Thirty-two, tall, solid, athletic,
          attractive
BERNARD   Twenty-eight, Negro, nice-
          looking
COWBOY   Twenty-two, light blond, muscle-
          bound, too pretty
HAROLD   Thirty-two, dark, lean, strong
          limbs, unusual Semitic face
ALAN   Thirty, aristocratic Anglo-Saxon
          features

The play is divided into two acts. The action is continuous and occurs one evening within the time necessary to perform the script.

Act 1

A smartly appointed duplex apartment in the East Fifties, New York, consisting of a living room and, on a higher level, a bedroom. Bossa nova music blasts from a phonograph.

MICHAEL, *wearing a robe, enters from the kitchen, carrying some liquor bottles. He crosses to set them on a bar, looks to see if the room is in order, moves toward the stairs to the bedroom level, doing a few improvised dance steps en route. In the bedroom, he crosses before a mirror, studies his hair—sighs. He picks up comb and a hair drier, goes to work.*

The downstairs front-door buzzer sounds. A beat. MICHAEL *stops, listens, turns off the drier. More buzzing.* MICHAEL *quickly goes to the living room, turns off the music, opens the door to reveal* DONALD, *dressed in khakis and a Lacoste shirt, carrying an airline zipper bag.*

MICHAEL
Donald! You're about a day and a half early!

DONALD
[*Enters*]
The doctor canceled!

MICHAEL
Canceled! How'd you get inside?

DONALD
The street door was open.

MICHAEL
You wanna drink?

DONALD
[*Going to bedroom to deposit his bag*]
Not until I've had my shower. I want something to work-out today—I want to try to relax and enjoy *something.*

MICHAEL
You in a blue funk because of the doctor?

DONALD
[*Returning*]
Christ, no. I was depressed long before I got *there.*

MICHAEL
Why'd the prick cancel?

DONALD
A virus or something. He looked awful.

MICHAEL
[*Holding up a shopping bag*]

Well, this'll pick you up. I went shopping today and bought all kind of goodies. Sandalwood soap . . .

DONALD
[*Removing his socks and shoes*]
I feel better already.

MICHAEL
[*Producing articles*]
. . . Your very own toothbrush because I'm sick to death of your using mine.

DONALD
How do you think *I* feel.

MICHAEL
You've had worse things in your mouth.
[*Holds up a cylindrical can*]
And, also for you . . . something called "Control." Notice nowhere is it called hair spray—just simply "Control." And the words "For Men" are written about thirty-seven times all over the goddamn can!

DONALD
It's called Butch Assurance.

MICHAEL
Well, it's *still* hair spray—no matter if they call it "*Balls*"!
[DONALD *laughs*]
It's all going on your very own shelf, which is to be labeled: Donald's Saturday Night Douche Kit. By the way, are you spending the night?

DONALD
Nope. I'm driving back. I still get very itchy when I'm in this town too long. I'm not that well yet.

MICHAEL
That's what you say every weekend.

DONALD
Maybe after about ten more years of analysis I'll be able to stay one night.

MICHAEL
Maybe after about ten more years of analysis you'll be able to move back to town permanently.

DONALD
If I live that long.

MICHAEL
You will. If you don't kill yourself on the Long Island Expressway some early Sunday morning. I'll never know how you can tank up on martinis and make it back to the Hamptons in one piece.

DONALD
Believe me, it's easier than getting here. Ever had an anxiety attack at sixty miles an hour? Well, tonight I was beside myself to get to the doctor—and just as I finally make it, rush in, throw myself on the couch, and vomit out how depressed I am, he says, "Donald, I have to cancel tonight—I'm just too sick."

MICHAEL
Why didn't you tell him you're sicker than he is.

DONALD
He already knows *that*.
[DONALD *goes to the bedroom, drops his shoes and socks.* MICHAEL *follows*]

MICHAEL
Why didn't the prick call you and cancel. Suppose

you'd driven all this way for nothing.

DONALD
[*Removing his shirt*]
Why do you keep calling him a prick?

MICHAEL
Whoever heard of an analyst having a session with a patient for two hours on Saturday evening.

DONALD
He simply prefers to take Mondays off.

MICHAEL
Works late on Saturday and takes Monday off—what is he, a psychiatrist or a hairdresser?

DONALD
Actually, he's both. He shrinks my head and combs me out.
[*Lies on the bed*]
Besides, I had to come in town to a birthday party anyway. Right?

MICHAEL
You had to remind me. If there's one thing I'm not ready for, it's five screaming queens singing Happy Birthday.

DONALD
Who's coming?

MICHAEL
They're really all Harold's friends. It's *his* birthday and I want everything to be just the way he'd want it. I don't want to have to listen to him kvetch about how nobody ever does anything for anybody but themselves.

DONALD
Himself.

MICHAEL
Himself. I think you know everybody anyway—they're
the same old tired fairies you've seen around since the
day one. Actually, there'll be seven, counting Harold
and you and me.

DONALD
Are you calling me a screaming queen or a tired fairy?

MICHAEL
Oh, I beg your pardon—six tired screaming fairy queens
and one anxious queer.

DONALD
You don't think Harold'll mind my being here, do you?
Technically, I'm *your* friend, not his.

MICHAEL
If she doesn't like it, she can twirl on it. Listen, I'll be
out of your way in just a second. I've only got one
more thing to do.

DONALD
Surgery, so early in the evening?

MICHAEL
Sunt! That's French, with a cedilla.
[*Gives him a crooked third finger, goes to mirror*]
I've just got to comb my hair for the thirty-seventh
time. Hair—that's singular. My hair, without exaggera-
tion, is clearly falling on the floor. And *fast,* baby!

DONALD
You're totally paranoid. You've got plenty of hair.

MICHAEL

What you see before you is a masterpiece of deception. My hairline starts about here.
[*Indicates his crown*]
All this is just tortured forward.

DONALD

Well, I hope, for your sake, no strong wind comes up.

MICHAEL

If one does, I'll be in terrible trouble. I will then have a bald head and shoulder-length fringe.
[*Runs his fingers through his hair, holds it away from his scalp, dips the top of his head so that* DONALD *can see.* DONALD *is silent*]
Not good, huh?

DONALD

Not the best.

MICHAEL

It's called, "getting old." Ah, life is such a grand de-sign—spring, summer, fall, winter, death. Who*ever* could have thought it up?

DONALD

No one *we* know, that's for sure.

MICHAEL

[*Turns to study himself in the mirror, sighs*]
Well, one thing you can say for masturbation . . . you certainly don't have to look your best.
[*Slips out of the robe, flings it at* DONALD. DONALD *laughs, takes the robe, exits to the bath.* MICHAEL *takes a sweater out of a chest, pulls it on*]

MICHAEL

What are you so depressed about? I mean, other than the usual *everything*.
　[*A beat*]

DONALD
　[*Reluctantly*]
I really don't want to get into it.

MICHAEL

Well, if you're not going to tell me, how can we have a conversation *in depth*—a warm, rewarding, meaningful friendship?

DONALD

Up yours!

MICHAEL
　[*Southern accent*]
Why, Cap'n Butler, how you talk!
　[*Pause.* DONALD *appears in the doorway holding a glass of water and a small bottle of pills.* MICHAEL *looks up*]

DONALD

It's just that today I finally realized that I was *raised* to be a failure. I was *groomed* for it.
　[*A beat*]

MICHAEL

You know, there was a time when you could have said that to me and I wouldn't have known what the hell you were talking about.

DONALD
　[*Takes some pills*]
Naturally, it all goes back to Evelyn and Walt.

MICHAEL

Naturally. When doesn't it go back to Mom and Pop.
Unfortunately, we all had an Evelyn and a Walt. The
crumbs! Don't you love that word—crumb? Oh, I love
it! It's a real Barbara Stanwyck word.

[*A la Stanwyck's frozen-lipped Brooklyn accent*]
"Cau'll me a keab, you kr-rumm."

DONALD

Well, I see all vestiges of sanity for this evening are
now officially shot to hell.

MICHAEL

Oh, Donald, you're so serious tonight! You're fun-
starved, baby, and I'm eating for two!

[*Sings*]
"Forget your troubles, c'mon get happy! You better
chase all your blues away. Shout, 'Hallelujah!' c'mon
get happy . . ."

[*Sees* DONALD *isn't buying it*]
—what's more boring than a queen doing a Judy Gar-
land imitation?

DONALD

A queen doing a Bette Davis imitation.

MICHAEL

Meanwhile—back at the Evelyn and Walt Syndrome.

DONALD

America's Square Peg and America's Round Hole.

MICHAEL

Christ, how sick analysts must get of hearing how
mommy and daddy made their darlin' into a fairy.

DONALD

It's beyond just that now. Today I finally began to see

how some of the other pieces of the puzzle relate to them.—Like why I never finished anything I started in my life . . . my neurotic compulsion to not succeed. I've realized it was always when I failed that Evelyn loved me the most—because it displeased Walt, who wanted perfection. And when I fell short of the mark she was only too happy to make up for it with her love. So I began to identify failing with winning my mother's love. And I began to fail on purpose to get it. I didn't finish Cornell—I couldn't keep a job in this town. I simply retreated to a room over a garage and scrubbing floors in order to keep alive. Failure is the only thing with which I feel at home. Because it is what I was taught at home.

MICHAEL

Killer whales is what they are. Killer whales. How many whales could a killer whale kill . . .

DONALD

A lot, especially if they get them when they were babies.
    [*Pause.* MICHAEL *suddenly tears off his sweater, throws it in the air, letting it land where it may, whips out another, pulls it on as he starts down the stairs for the living room.* DONALD *follows*]
Hey! Where're you going?

MICHAEL

To make drinks! I think we need about thirty-seven!

DONALD

Where'd you get *that* sweater?

MICHAEL

This clever little shop on the right bank called Hermes.

DONALD

I work my ass off for forty-five lousy dollars a week

scrubbing floors and you waltz around throwing cash-mere sweaters on them.

MICHAEL
The one on the floor in the bedroom is vicuña.

DONALD
I *beg* your pardon.

MICHAEL
You could get a job doing something else. Nobody holds a gun to your head to be a charwoman. That is, how you say, your neurosis.

DONALD
Gee, and I thought it's why I was born.

MICHAEL
Besides, just because I *wear* expensive clothes doesn't necessarily mean they're paid for.

DONALD
That is, how you say, *your* neurosis.

MICHAEL
I'm a spoiled brat, so what do I know about being mature. The only thing mature means to me is *Victor* Mature, who was in all those pictures with Betty Grable.
[*Sings à la Grable*]
"I can't begin to tell you, how much you mean to me . . ." Betty sang that in 1945. '45?—'43. No, '43 was "Coney Island," which was remade in '50 as "Wabash Avenue." Yes, "Dolly Sisters" was in '45.

DONALD
How did I manage to miss these momentous events in the American cinema. I can understand people having

an affinity for the stage—but movies are such garbage, who can take them seriously.

MICHAEL

Well, I'm sorry if your sense of art is offended. Odd as it may seem, there wasn't any Shubert Theatre in Hot Coffee, Mississippi!

DONALD

However—thanks to the silver screen, your neurosis has got style. It takes a certain flair to squander one's unemployment check at Pavillion.

MICHAEL

What's so snappy about being head over heels in debt. The only thing smart about it is the ingenious ways I dodge the bill collectors.

DONALD

Yeah. Come to think of it, you're the type that gives faggots a bad name.

MICHAEL

And you, Donald, *you* are a credit to the homosexual. A reliable, hard-working, floor-scrubbing, bill-paying fag who don't owe nothin' to nobody.

DONALD

I am a model fairy.

> [MICHAEL *has taken some ribbon and paper and begun to wrap* HAROLD's *birthday gift*]

MICHAEL

You think it's just nifty how I've always flitted from Beverly Hills to Rome to Acapulco to Amsterdam, picking up a lot of one-night stands and a lot of custom-made duds along the trail, but I'm here to tell you that the only place in all those miles—the only place

I've ever been *happy*—was on the goddamn plane.

[*Puffs up the bow on the package, continues*]

Bored with Scandinavia, try Greece. Fed up with dark meat, try light. Hate tequila, what about slivovitz. Tired of boys, what about girls—or how about boys and girls mixed and in what combination? And if you're sick of people, what about poppers? Or pot or pills or the hard stuff. And can you think of anything else the bad baby would like to indulge his spoiled-rotten, stupid, empty, boring, selfish, self-centered self in? Is that what you think has style, Donald? Huh? Is that what you think you've missed out on—my hysterical escapes from country to country, party to party, bar to bar, bed to bed, hangover to hangover, and all of it, hand to mouth!

[*A beat*]

Run, charge, run, buy, borrow, make, spend, run, squander, beg, run, run, run, waste, waste, *waste!*

[*A beat*]

And why? And why?

DONALD

Why, Michael? Why?

MICHAEL

I really don't want to get into it.

DONALD

Then how can we have a conversation in depth?

MICHAEL

Oh, you know it all by heart anyway. Same song, second verse. Because my Evelyn refused to let me grow up. She was determined to keep me a child forever and she did one helluva job of it. And my Walt stood by and let her do it.

[*A beat*]

What you see before you is a thirty-year-old infant. And it was all done in the name of love—what *she* labeled love and probably sincerely believed to be love, when what she was really doing was feeding her own need—satisfying her own loneliness.

[*A beat*]

She made me into a girl-friend dash lover.

[*A beat*]

We went to all those goddamn cornball movies together. I picked out her clothes for her and told her what to wear and she'd take me to the beauty parlor with her and we'd both get our hair bleached and a permanent and a manicure.

[*A beat*]

And Walt let this happen.

[*A beat*]

And she convinced me that I was a sickly child who couldn't run and play and sweat and get knocked around—oh, no! I was frail and pale and, to hear her tell it, practically female. I can't tell you the thousands of times she said to me, "I declare, Michael, you should have been a girl." And I guess I should have—I was frail and pale and bleached and curled and bedded down with hot-water bottles and my dolls and my paper dolls, and my doll clothes and my doll houses!

[*Quick beat*]

And Walt bought them for me!

[*Beat. With increasing speed*]

And she nursed me and put Vicks salve on my chest and cold cream on my face and told me what beautiful eyes I had and what pretty lips I had. She bathed me in the same tub with her until I grew too big for the two of us to fit. She made me sleep in the same bed with her until I was fourteen years old—until I finally flatly refused to spend one more night there. She didn't want to prepare me for life or how to be out in the world on my own or I might have left her. But I left anyway. This goddamn cripple finally wrenched free and limped away. And here I am—unequipped, undisciplined, untrained, unprepared and unable to live!

[*A beat*]
And do you know until this day she still says, "I don't care if you're seventy years old, you'll always be my baby." And can I tell you how that drives me mad! Will that bitch never understand that what I'll always *be* is her son—but that I haven't been her baby for twenty-five years!

[*A beat*]
And don't get me wrong. I know it's easy to cop out and blame Evelyn and Walt and say it was *their* fault. That we were simply the helpless put-upon victims. But in the end, we are responsible for ourselves. And I guess—I'm not sure—but I want to believe it—that in their own pathetic, *dangerous* way, they just loved us too much.

[*A beat*]
Finis. Applause.

[DONALD *hesitates, walks over to* MICHAEL, *puts his arms around him and holds him. It is a totally warm and caring gesture*]

There's nothing quite as good as feeling sorry for yourself, is there?

DONALD
Nothing.

MICHAEL
[*A la Bette Davis*]
I adore cheap sentiment.
[*Breaks away*]
Okay, I'm taking orders for drinks. What'll it be?

DONALD
An extra-dry-Beefeater-martini-on-the-rocks-with-a-twist.

MICHAEL
Coming up.

[DONALD *exits up the stairs into the bath;* MICHAEL *into the kitchen.*

Momentarily, MICHAEL *returns, carrying an ice bucket in one hand and a silver tray of cracked crab in the other, singing "Acapulco" or "Down Argentine Way" or some other forgotten Grable tune.*

The telephone rings]

MICHAEL
[*Answering it*]
Backstage, "New Moon."
[*A beat*]
Alan? My God, I don't believe it. How *are* you? *Where* are you? In town! Great! When'd you get in? Is Fran with you? Oh. What? No. No, I'm tied up tonight. No, tonight's no good for me. —You mean, *now?* Well, Alan, ole boy, it's a friend's birthday and I'm having a few people. —No, you wouldn't exactly call it a birthday party—well, yes, actually I guess you would. I mean, what else would you call it. A *wake*, maybe. I'm sorry I can't ask you to join us—but—well, kiddo, it just wouldn't work out. —No, it's not place cards or anything. It's just that—well, I'd hate to just see you for ten minutes and . . . Alan? Alan? What's the matter? —Are you—are you crying? —Oh, Alan, what's wrong? —Alan, listen, come on over. No, no, it's perfectly all right. Well, just hurry up. I mean, come on by and have a drink, okay? Alan . . . are you all right? Okay. Yeah. Same old address. Yeah. Bye.

[*Slowly hangs up, stares blankly into space.* DONALD *appears, bathed and changed. He strikes a pose*]

DONALD
Well. Am I stunning?
[MICHAEL *looks up*]

MICHAEL
[*Tonelessly*]

[34]

You're absolutely stunning. —You *look* like shit, but I'm
absolutely stunned.

DONALD
    [*Crestfallen*]
Your grapes are, how you say, sour.

MICHAEL
Listen, you won't believe what just happened.

DONALD
Where's my drink?

MICHAEL
I didn't make it—I've been on the phone.
    [DONALD *goes to the bar, makes himself a martini*]

MICHAEL
My old roommate from Georgetown just called.

DONALD
Alan what's-his-name?

MICHAEL
McCarthy. He's up here from Washington on business
or something and he's on his way over here.

DONALD
Well, I hope he knows the lyrics to Happy Birthday.

MICHAEL
Listen, asshole, what am I going to do? He's *straight*.
And *Square City!*
    [*"Top Drawer" accent through clenched teeth*]
I mean, he's rally vury proper. Auffully good family.

DONALD
    [*Same accent*]
That's *so* important.

MICHAEL
    [*Regular speech*]
I mean, they look down on people in the *theatre*—so whatta you think he'll feel about this *freak show* I've got booked for dinner?

DONALD
    [*Sipping his drink*]
Christ, is that good.

MICHAEL
Want some cracked crab?

DONALD
Not just yet. Why'd you invite him over?

MICHAEL
He invited himself. He said he had to see me tonight. *Immediately*. He absolutely lost his spring on the phone—started crying.

DONALD
Maybe he's feeling sorry for himself too.

MICHAEL
Great heaves and sobs. Really boo-hoo-hoo-time—and that's not his style at all. I mean, he's so pulled-together he wouldn't show any emotion if he were in a plane crash. What am I going to do?

DONALD
What the hell do you care what he thinks.

MICHAEL
Well, I don't really but . . .

DONALD
Or are you suddenly ashamed of your friends?

MICHAEL

Donald, *you* are the only person I know of whom I am truly ashamed. Some people *do* have different standards from yours and mine, you know. And if we don't acknowledge them, we're just as narrow-minded and backward as we think they are.

DONALD

You know what you are, Michael? You're a *real* person.

MICHAEL

Thank you and fuck you.
    [MICHAEL *crosses to take a piece of crab and nibble on it*]
Want some?

DONALD

No, thanks. How could you ever have been friends with a bore like that?

MICHAEL

Believe it or not, there was a time in my life when I didn't go around *announcing* that I was a faggot.

DONALD

That must have been before speech replaced sign language.

MICHAEL

Don't give me any static on that score. I didn't come out until I left college.

DONALD

It seems to me that the first time we tricked we met in a gay bar on Third Avenue during your *junior* year.

MICHAEL

Cunt.

DONALD
I thought you'd never say it.

MICHAEL
Sure you don't want any cracked crab?

DONALD
Not yet! If you don't mind!

MICHAEL
Well, it can only be getting colder. What time is it?

DONALD
I don't know. Early.

MICHAEL
Where the hell is Alan?

DONALD
Do you want some more club soda?

MICHAEL
What?

DONALD
There's nothing but club soda in that glass. It's not gin
—like mine. You want some more?

MICHAEL
No.

DONALD
I've been watching you for several Saturdays now.
You've actually stopped drinking, haven't you?

MICHAEL
And smoking too.

[38]

DONALD
And smoking too. How long's it been?

MICHAEL
Five weeks.

DONALD
That's amazing.

MICHAEL
I've found God.

DONALD
It *is* amazing—for you.

MICHAEL
Or is God dead?

DONALD
Yes, thank God. And don't get panicky just because I'm paying you a compliment. I can tell the difference.

MICHAEL
You always said that I held my liquor better than anybody you ever saw.

DONALD
I could always tell when you were getting high—one way.

MICHAEL
I'd get hostile.

DONALD
You seem happier or something now—and that shows.

MICHAEL
[*Quietly*]

Thanks.

DONALD
What made you stop—the analyst?

MICHAEL
He certainly had a lot to do with it. Mainly, I just didn't think I could survive another hangover, that's all. I don't think I could get through that morning-after ick attack.

DONALD
Morning-after what?

MICHAEL
Icks! Anxiety! Guilt! Unfathomable guilt—either real or imagined—from that split second your eyes pop open and you say, "Oh, my God, what did I do last night!" and ZAP, Total recall!

DONALD
Tell me about it!

MICHAEL
Then, the coffee, aspirin, Alka-Seltzer, Darvon, Daprisal, and a quick call to I.A.—Icks Anonymous.

DONALD
"Good morning, I.A."

MICHAEL
"Hi! Was I too bad last night? Did I do anything wrong? I didn't do anything terrible, did I?"

DONALD
[*Laughing*]
How many times! How many times!

MICHAEL

And from then on, that struggle to live till lunch, when you have a double Bloody Mary—that is, if you've *waited* until lunch—and then you're half pissed again and useless for the rest of the afternoon. And the only sure cure is to go to bed for about thirty-seven hours, but who ever does that. Instead, you hang on till cocktail time, and by then you're ready for what the night holds—which hopefully is another party, where the whole goddamn cycle starts over!

[*A beat*]

Well, I've been on that merry-go-round long enough and I either had to get off or die of centrifugal force.

DONALD

And just how does a clear head stack up with the dull fog of alcohol?

MICHAEL

Well, all those things you've always heard are true. Nothing can compare with the experience of one's faculties functioning at their maximum natural capacity. The only thing is . . . I'd *kill* for a drink.

[*The wall-panel buzzer sounds*]

DONALD

Joe College has finally arrived.

MICHAEL

Suddenly, I have such an ick!

[*Presses the wall-panel button*]

Now listen, Donald . . .

DONALD

[*Quick*]

Michael, don't insult me by giving me any lecture on acceptable social behavior. I promise to sit with my legs spread apart and keep my voice in a deep register.

MICHAEL

Donald, you are a real *card-carrying cunt.*

[*The apartment door buzzes several times.* MI-
CHAEL *goes to it, pauses briefly before it, tears it
open to reveal* EMORY, LARRY *and* HANK. EMORY *is
in Bermuda shorts and a sweater.* LARRY *has on a
turtleneck and sandals.* HANK *is in a dark Ivy
League suit with a vest and has on cordovan shoes.*
LARRY *and* HANK *carry birthday gifts.* EMORY *carries a large covered dish*]

EMORY

[*Bursting in*]

ALL RIGHT THIS IS A RAID! EVERYBODY'S UN-
DER ARREST!

[*This entrance is followed by a loud raucous laugh
as* EMORY *throws his arms around* MICHAEL *and
gives him a big kiss on the cheek. Referring to
dish*]

Hello, darlin'! Connie Casserole. Oh, Mary, don't ask.

MICHAEL

[*Weary already*]

Hello, Emory. Put it in the kitchen.

[EMORY *spots* DONALD]

EMORY

Who is this exotic woman over here?

MICHAEL

Hi, Hank. Larry.

[*They say, "Hi," shake hands, enter.* MICHAEL *looks
out in the hall, comes back into the room, closes
the door*]

DONALD

Hi, Emory.

EMORY

My dear, I thought you had perished! Where have you been hiding your classically chiseled features?

DONALD
    [*To* EMORY]
I don't live in the city any more.

MICHAEL
    [*To* LARRY *and* HANK, *referring to the gifts*]
Here, I'll take those. Where's yours, Emory?

EMORY

It's arriving later.
    [EMORY *exits to the kitchen.* LARRY *and* DONALD'S
    eyes have met. HANK *has handed* MICHAEL *his gift*
    —LARRY *is too preoccupied*]

HANK

Larry!—Larry!

LARRY

What!

HANK

Give Michael the gift!

LARRY

Oh. Here.
    [*To* HANK]
Louder. So my mother in Philadelphia can hear you.

HANK

Well, you were just standing there in a trance.

MICHAEL
    [*To* LARRY *and* HANK *as* EMORY *reenters*]
You both know Donald, don't you?

[43]

DONALD
Sure. Nice to see you.
    [*To* HANK]
Hi.

HANK
    [*Shaking hands*]
Nice to meet you.

MICHAEL
Oh, I thought you'd met.

DONALD
Well . . .

LARRY
We haven't exactly met but we've . . . Hi.

DONALD
Hi.

HANK
But you've what?

LARRY
. . . *Seen* . . . each other before.

MICHAEL
Well, *that* sounds murky.

HANK
You've never met but you've seen each other.

LARRY
What was wrong with the way *I* said it.

HANK
Where?

EMORY
    [*Loud aside to* MICHAEL]
I think they're going to have their first fight.

LARRY
The first one since we got out of the taxi.

MICHAEL
    [*Referring to* EMORY]
Where'd you find this trash.

LARRY
Downstairs leaning against a lamppost.

EMORY
With an orchid behind my ear and big wet lips painted over the lipline.

MICHAEL
Just like Maria Montez.

DONALD
Oh, *please!*

EMORY
    [*To* DONALD]
What have you got against Maria—she was a good woman.

MICHAEL
Listen, everybody, this old college friend of mine is in town and he's stopping by for a fast drink on his way to dinner somewhere. But, listen, he's *straight,* so . . .

LARRY
Straight! If it's the one I met, he's about as straight as the Yellow Brick Road.

MICHAEL
No, you met Justin Stuart.

HANK
I don't remember anybody named Justin Stuart.

LARRY
Of course you don't, dope. *I* met him.

MICHAEL
Well, this is someone else.

DONALD
Alan McCarthy. A very close total stranger.

MICHAEL
It's not that I care what he would think of me, really—
it's just that *he's* not ready for it. And he never will be.
You understand that, don't you, Hank?

HANK
Oh, sure.

LARRY
You honestly think he doesn't know about you?

MICHAEL
If there's the slightest suspicion, he's never let on one
bit.

EMORY
What's he had, a lobotomy?
    [*He exits up the stairs into the bath*]

MICHAEL
I was super-careful when I was in college and I still am
whenever I see him. I don't know why, but I am.

DONALD
Tilt.

MICHAEL
You may think it was a crock of shit, Donald, but to him I'm sure we were close friends. The closest. To pop that balloon now just wouldn't be fair to him. Isn't that right?

LARRY
Whatever's fair.

MICHAEL
Well, of course. And if that's phony of me, Donald, then that's phony of me and make something of it.

DONALD
I pass.

MICHAEL
Well, even you have to admit it's much simpler to deal with the world according to its rules and then go right ahead and do what you damn well please. You do understand *that*, don't you?

DONALD
Now that you've put it in layman's terms.

MICHAEL
I was just like Alan when I was in college. Very large in the dating department. Wore nothing but those constipated Ivy League clothes and those ten-pound cordovan shoes.
    [*To* HANK]
No offense.

HANK
Quite all right.

MICHAEL

I butched it up quite a bit. And I didn't think I was lying to myself. I really thought I was straight.

EMORY

[*Coming downstairs tucking a Kleenex into his sleeve*]
Who do you have to fuck to get a drink around here?

MICHAEL

Will you *light* somewhere?
    [EMORY *sits on steps*]
Or I thought I thought I was straight. I know I didn't come out till after I'd graduated.

DONALD

What about all those weekends up from school?

MICHAEL

I still wasn't out. I was still in the "Christ-was-I-drunk-last-night syndrome."

LARRY

The *what?*

MICHAEL

The Christ-was-I-drunk-last-night syndrome. You know, when you made it with some guy in school and the next day when you had to face each other there was always a lot of shit-kicking crap about, "Man, was I drunk last night! Christ, I don't remember a thing!"
    [*Everyone laughs*]

DONALD

You were just guilty because you were Catholic, that's all.

MICHAEL

That's not true. The Christ-was-I-drunk-last-night syn-

drome knows no religion. It has to do with immaturity.
Although I will admit there's a high percentage of it
among Mormons.

EMORY
Trollop.

MICHAEL
We all somehow managed to justify our actions in those
days. I later found out that even Justin Stuart, my closest friend . . .

DONALD
Other than Alan McCarthy.

MICHAEL
[*A look to* DONALD]
. . . was doing the same thing. Only Justin was going
to Boston on weekends.
[EMORY *and* LARRY *laugh*]

LARRY
[*To* HANK]
Sound familiar?

MICHAEL
Yes, long before Justin or I or God only knows how
many others *came out,* we used to get drunk and "horse
around" a bit. You see, in the Christ-was-I-drunk-last-
night syndrome, you really *are* drunk. That part of it is
true. It's just that you also *do remember everything.*
[*General laughter*]
Oh God, I used to have to get loaded to go in a gay bar!

DONALD
Well, times certainly have changed.

MICHAEL
They *have.* Lately I've gotten to despise the bars.

Everybody just standing around and standing around
—it's like one eternal intermission.

HANK
[*To* LARRY]
Sound familiar?

EMORY
I can't stand the bars either. All that cat-and-mouse
business—you hang around *staring* at each other all
night and wind up going home alone.

MICHAEL
And pissed.

LARRY
A lot of guys have to get loaded to have sex.
[*Quick look to* HANK, *who is unamused*]
So I've been told.

MICHAEL
If you remember, Donald, the first time we made it I
was so drunk I could hardly stand up.

DONALD
You were so drunk you could hardly *get* it up.

MICHAEL
[*Mock innocence*]
Christ, I was so drunk I don't remember.

DONALD
Bullshit, you remember.

MICHAEL
[*Sings to* DONALD]
"Just friends, lovers no more . . ."

EMORY
You may as well be. Everybody thinks you are anyway.

DONALD
We never *were—really*.

MICHAEL
We didn't have time to be—we got to know each other
too fast.
    [*Door buzzer sounds*]
Oh, Jesus, it's Alan! Now, please everybody, do me a
favor and cool it for the few minutes he's here.

EMORY
Anything for a sis, Mary.

MICHAEL
That's *exactly* what I'm talking about, Emory. *No
camping!*

EMORY
Sorry.
    [*Deep, deep voice to* DONALD]
Think the Giants are gonna win the pennant this year?

DONALD
    [*Deep, deep voice*]
Fuckin' A, Mac.
    [MICHAEL *goes to the door, opens it to reveal* BER-
    NARD, *dressed in a shirt and tie and sport jacket.
    He carries a birthday gift and two bottles of red
    wine*]

EMORY
    [*Big scream*]
Oh, it's only another queen!

BERNARD
And it ain't the Red one, either.

EMORY
It's the queen of spades!
[BERNARD *enters.* MICHAEL *looks out in the hall*]

MICHAEL
Bernard, is the downstairs door open?

BERNARD
It was, but I closed it.

MICHAEL
Good.
[BERNARD *starts to put wine on bar*]

MICHAEL
[*Referring to the two bottles of red wine*]
I'll take those. You can put your present with the others.
[MICHAEL *closes the door.* BERNARD *hands him the gift. The phone rings*]

BERNARD
Hi, Larry. Hi, Hank.

MICHAEL
Christ of the Andes! Donald, will you bartend please.
[MICHAEL *gives* DONALD *the wine bottles, goes to the phone*]

BERNARD
[*Extending his hand to* DONALD]
Hello, Donald. Good to see you.

DONALD
Bernard.

MICHAEL
    [*Answers phone*]
Hello? Alan?

EMORY
Hi, Bernardette. Anybody ever tell you you'd look divine in a hammock, surrounded by louvres and ceiling fans and lots and lots of lush tropical ferns?

BERNARD
    [*To* EMORY]
You're *such* a fag. You take the cake.

EMORY
Oh, what *about* the cake—whose job was that?

LARRY
Mine. I ordered one to be delivered.

EMORY
How many candles did you say put on it—eighty?

MICHAEL
. . . What? Wait a minute. There's too much noise. Let me go to another phone.
    [*Presses the hold button, hangs up, dashes toward stairs*]

LARRY
Michael, did the cake come?

MICHAEL
No.

DONALD
    [*To* MICHAEL *as he passes*]
What's up?

MICHAEL
Do *I* know?

LARRY
Jesus, I'd better call. Okay if I use the private line?

MICHAEL
[*Going upstairs*]
Sure.
[*Stops dead on stairs, turns*]
Listen, everybody, there's some cracked crab there.
Help yourselves.
[DONALD *shakes his head.* MICHAEL *continues up the stairs to the bedroom.* LARRY *crosses to the phone, presses the free-line button, picks up receiver, dials Information*]

DONALD
Is everybody ready for a drink?
[HANK *and* BERNARD *say,* "Yeah"]

EMORY
[*Flipping up his sweater*]
Ready! I'll be your topless cocktail waitress.

BERNARD
Please spare us the sight of your sagging tits.

EMORY
[*To* HANK, LARRY]
What're you having, kids?

MICHAEL
[*Having picked up the bedside phone*]
... Yes, Alan ...

LARRY
Vodka and tonic.

[*Into phone*]
Could I have the number for the Marseilles Bakery in
Manhattan.

EMORY
A vod and ton and a . . .

HANK
Is there any beer?

EMORY
Beer! Who drinks beer before dinner?

BERNARD
Beer drinkers.

DONALD
That's telling him.

MICHAEL
. . . No, Alan, don't be silly. What's there to apologize
for?

EMORY
Truck drivers do. Or . . . or wallpaperers. Not school
teachers. They have sherry.

HANK
This one has beer.

EMORY
Well, maybe school teachers in *public* schools.
    [*To* LARRY]
How can a sensitive artist like you live with an insensi-
tive bull like that?

LARRY
    [*Hanging up the phone and redialing*]
I can't.

BERNARD

Emory, you'd live with Hank in a minute, if he'd ask you. In fifty-eight seconds. Lord knows, you're *sssen-sitive.*

EMORY

Why don't you have a piece of watermelon and hush up!

MICHAEL

. . . Alan, don't be ridiculous.

DONALD

Here you go, Hank.

HANK

Thanks.

LARRY

Shit. They don't answer.

DONALD

What're you having, Emory?

BERNARD

A Pink Lady.

EMORY

A vodka martini on the rocks, please.

LARRY

[*Hangs up*]

Well, let's just hope.

[DONALD *hands* LARRY *his drink—their eyes meet again. A faint smile crosses* LARRY'S *lips.* DONALD *returns to the bar to make* EMORY'S *drink*]

MICHAEL
Lunch tomorrow will be great. One o'clock—the Oak Room at the Plaza okay? Fine.

BERNARD
[*To* DONALD]
Donald, read any new libraries lately?

DONALD
One or three. I did the complete works of Doris Lessing this week. I've been depressed.

MICHAEL
Alan, forget it, will you? Right. Bye.
[*Hangs up, starts to leave the room—stops. Quickly pulls off the sweater he is wearing, takes out another, crosses to the stairs*]

DONALD
You must not work in Circulation any more.

BERNARD
Oh, I'm still there—every day.

DONALD
Well, since I moved, I only come in on Saturday evenings.
[*Moves his stack of books off the bar*]

HANK
Looks like you stock up for the week.
[MICHAEL *rises and crosses to steps landing*]

BERNARD
Are you kidding—that'll last him two days.

EMORY
It would last *me* two years. I still haven't finished *Atlas*

[57]

Shrugged, which I started in 1912.

MICHAEL
    [*To* DONALD]
Well, he's not coming.

DONALD
It's just as well now.

BERNARD
Some people eat, some people drink, some take dope . . .

DONALD
I read.

MICHAEL
And read and read and read. It's a wonder your eyes
don't turn back in your head at the sight of a dust
jacket.

HANK
Well, at least he's a constructive escapist.

MICHAEL
Yeah, what do I do—take planes. No, I don't do that
any more. Because I don't have the *money* to do that
any more. I go to the baths. That's about it.

EMORY
I'm about to do both. I'm flying to the West Coast—

BERNARD
You still have that act with a donkey in Tijuana?

EMORY
I'm going to *San Francisco* on a well-earned vacation.

[MICHAEL *starts for bar*]

DONALD
I'll get it.
[*Goes to bar*]

HANK
[*Forced laugh*]
Guess I'm the only beer drinker.

ALAN
[*Looking around group*]
Whose . . . birthday . . . is it?

LARRY
Harold's.

ALAN
[*Looking from face to face*]
Harold?

BERNARD
He's not here yet.

EMORY
She's never been on time . . .
[MICHAEL *shoots* EMORY *a withering glance*]
He's never been on time in his . . .

MICHAEL
Alan's from Washington. We went to college together.
Georgetown.
[*A beat. Silence*]

EMORY
Well, isn't that fascinating.
[DONALD *hands* ALAN *his drink*]

DONALD
If that's too strong, I'll put some water in it.

ALAN
[*Takes a quick gulp*]
It's fine. Thanks. Fine.

HANK
Are you in the government?

ALAN
No. I'm a lawyer. What . . . what do you do?

HANK
I teach school.

ALAN
Oh. I would have taken you for an athlete of some sort.
You look like you might play sports . . . of some sort.

HANK
Well, I'm no professional but I was on the basketball
team in college and I play quite a bit of tennis.

ALAN
I play tennis too.

HANK
Great game.

ALAN
Yes. Great.
[*A beat. Silence*]
What . . . do you teach?

HANK
Math.

ALAN
Math?

HANK
Yes.

ALAN
Math. Well.

EMORY
Kinda makes you want to rush out and buy a slide rule, doesn't it?

MICHAEL
Emory. I'm going to need some help with dinner and you're elected. Come on!

EMORY
I'm *always* elected.

BERNARD
You're a natural-born domestic.

EMORY
Said the African queen! You come on, too—you can fan me while I make the salad dressing.

MICHAEL
    [*Glaring. Phony smile*]
RIGHT THIS WAY, EMORY!
    [MICHAEL *pushes the swinging door aside for* EMORY *and* BERNARD *to enter. They do and he follows. The door swings closed, and the muffled sound of* MICHAEL's *voice can be heard*]
    [*Offstage*]
You son-of-a-bitch!

EMORY
[*Offstage*]
What the hell do you want from me?

HANK
Why don't we all sit down.

ALAN
... Sure.
[HANK *and* ALAN *sit on the couch.* LARRY *crosses to the bar, refills his drink.* DONALD *comes over to refill his*]

LARRY
Hi.

DONALD
... Hi.

ALAN
I really feel terrible—barging in on you fellows this way.

LARRY
[*To* DONALD]
How've you been?

DONALD
Fine, thanks.

HANK
[*To* ALAN]
... Oh, that's okay.

DONALD
[*To* LARRY]
... And you?

LARRY
Oh . . . just fine.

ALAN
[*To* HANK]
You're married?
[LARRY *hears this, turns to look in the direction of
the couch.* MICHAEL *enters from the kitchen*]

HANK
[*Watching* LARRY *and* DONALD]
What?

ALAN
I see you're married.
[*Points to* HANK's *wedding band*]

HANK
Oh.

MICHAEL
[*Glaring at* DONALD]
Yes. Hank's married.

ALAN
You have any kids?

HANK
Yes. Two. A boy nine, and a girl seven. You should see
my boy play tennis—really puts his dad to shame.

DONALD
[*Avoiding* MICHAEL's *eyes*]
I better get some ice.
[*Exits to the kitchen*]

ALAN
[*To* HANK]

I have two kids too. Both girls.

HANK
Great.

MICHAEL
How *are* the girls, Alan?

ALAN
Oh, just sensational.
[*Shakes his head*]
They're something, those kids. God, I'm nuts about
them.

HANK
How long have you been married?

ALAN
Nine years. Can you believe it, Mickey?

MICHAEL
No.

ALAN
Mickey used to go with my wife when we were all in
school.

MICHAEL
Can you believe that?

ALAN
[*To* HANK]
You live in the city?

LARRY
Yes, we do.
[LARRY *comes over to couch next to* HANK]

ALAN
Oh.

HANK
I'm in the process of getting a divorce. Larry and I are
—roommates.

MICHAEL
Yes.

ALAN
Oh. I'm sorry. Oh, I mean . . .

HANK
I understand.

ALAN
   [Gets up]
I . . . I . . . I think I'd like another drink . . . If I may.

MICHAEL
Of course. What was it?

ALAN
I'll do it . . . if I may.
   *[Gets up, starts for the bar. Suddenly there is a
   loud crash offstage.* ALAN *jumps, looks toward
   swinging door]*
What was that?
   *[*DONALD *enters with the ice bucket]*

MICHAEL
Excuse me. Testy temperament out in the kitch!
   *[*MICHAEL *exits through the swinging door.* ALAN
   continues to the bar—starts nervously picking up
   and putting down bottles, searching for the
   Scotch]*

HANK
[*To* LARRY]
Larry, where do you know that guy from?

LARRY
What guy?

HANK
That guy.

LARRY
I don't know. Around. The bars.

DONALD
Can I help you, Alan?

ALAN
I . . . I can't seem to find the Scotch.

DONALD
You've got it in your hand.

ALAN
Oh. Of course. How . . . stupid of me.
[DONALD *watches* ALAN *fumble with the Scotch bottle and glass*]

DONALD
Why don't you let me do that.

ALAN
[*Gratefully hands him both*]
Thanks.

DONALD
Was it water or soda?

ALAN
Just make it straight—over ice.
  [MICHAEL *enters*]

MICHAEL
You see, Alan, I told you it wasn't a good time to talk.
But we . . .

ALAN
It doesn't matter. I'll just finish this and go . . .
  [*Takes a long swallow*]

LARRY
Where can Harold be?

MICHAEL
Oh, he's always late. You know how neurotic he is
about going out in public. It takes him hours to get
ready.

LARRY
Why *is* that?
  [EMORY *breezes in with an apron tied around his
  waist, carrying a stack of plates which he places
  on a drop-leaf table.* MICHAEL *does an eye roll*]

EMORY
Why is what?

LARRY
Why does Harold spend hours getting ready before he
can go out?

EMORY
Because she's a sick lady, that's why.
  [*Exits to the kitchen.* ALAN *finishes his drink*]

[73]

MICHAEL
Alan, as I was about to say, we can go in the bedroom
and talk.

ALAN
It really doesn't matter.

MICHAEL
Come on. Bring your drink.

ALAN
I . . . I've finished it.

MICHAEL
Well, make another and bring it upstairs.
[DONALD *picks up the Scotch bottle and pours into
the glass* ALAN *has in his hand.* MICHAEL *has started for the stairs*]

ALAN
[*To* DONALD]
Thanks.

DONALD
Don't mention it.

ALAN
[*To* HANK]
Excuse us. We'll be down in a minute.

LARRY
He'll still be here.
[*A beat*]

MICHAEL
[*On the stairs*]
Go ahead, Alan. I'll be right there.
[ALAN *turns awkwardly, exits to the bedroom.* MI-

CHAEL *goes into the kitchen. A beat*]

HANK
[*To* LARRY]
What was *that* supposed to mean?

LARRY
What was what supposed to mean?

HANK
You know.

LARRY
You want another beer?

HANK
No. You're jealous, aren't you?
[HANK *starts to laugh.* LARRY *doesn't like it*]

LARRY
I'm Larry. *You're* jealous.
[*Crosses to* DONALD]
Hey, Donald, where've you been hanging out these days? I haven't seen you in a long time . . .
[MICHAEL *enters to witness this disapprovingly. He turns, goes up the stairs.*
In the bedroom ALAN *is sitting on the edge of the bed.* MICHAEL *enters, pauses at the mirror to adjust his hair.*
Downstairs, HANK *gets up, exits into the kitchen.* DONALD *and* LARRY *move to a corner of the room, sit facing upstage and talk quietly*]

ALAN
[*To* MICHAEL]
This is a marvelous apartment.

MICHAEL

It's too expensive. I work to pay rent.

ALAN

What are you doing these days?

MICHAEL

Nothing.

ALAN

Aren't you writing any more?

MICHAEL

I haven't looked at a typewriter since I sold the very very wonderful, very very marvelous *screenplay* which never got produced.

ALAN

That's right. The last time I saw you, you were on your way to California. Or was it Europe?

MICHAEL

Hollywood. Which is not in Europe, nor does it have anything whatsoever to do with California.

ALAN

I've never been there but I would imagine it's awful. Everyone must be terribly cheap.

MICHAEL

No, not everyone.
     [ALAN *laughs. A beat.* MICHAEL *sits on the bed*]
Alan, I want to try to explain this evening . . .

ALAN

What's there to explain? Sometimes you just can't invite everybody to every party and some people take it personally. But I'm not one of them. I should apologize for inviting myself.

MICHAEL
That's not exactly what I meant.

ALAN
Your friends all seem like very nice guys. That Hank is really a very attractive fellow.

MICHAEL
. . . Yes. He is.

ALAN
We have a lot in common. What's his roommate's name?

MICHAEL
Larry.

ALAN
What does *he* do?

MICHAEL
He's a commercial artist.

ALAN
I liked Donald too. The only one I didn't care too much for was—what's his name—Emory?

MICHAEL
Yes. Emory.

ALAN
I just can't stand that kind of talk. It just grates on me.

MICHAEL
What kind of talk, Alan?

ALAN

Oh, you know. His brand of humor, I guess.

MICHAEL

He can be really quite funny sometimes.

ALAN

I suppose so. If you find that sort of thing amusing. He just seems like such a goddamn little pansy.
[*Silence. A pause*]
I'm sorry I said that. I didn't mean to say that. That's such an awful thing to say about *anyone*. But you know what I mean, Michael—you have to admit he *is* effeminate.

MICHAEL

He is a bit.

ALAN

A bit! He's like a . . . a butterfly in heat! I mean, there's no wonder he was trying to teach you all a dance. He *probably* wanted to dance *with* you!
[*Pause*]
Oh, come on, man, you know me—you know how I feel—your private life is your own affair.

MICHAEL
[*Icy*]
No. I *don't* know that about you.

ALAN

I couldn't care less what people do—as long as they don't do it in public—or—or try to force their ways on the whole damned world.

MICHAEL

Alan, what was it you were crying about on the telephone?

ALAN

Oh, I feel like such a fool about that. I could shoot myself for letting myself act that way. I'm so embarrassed I could die.

MICHAEL

But, Alan, if you were genuinely upset—that's nothing to be embarrassed about.

ALAN

All I can say is—please accept my apology for making such an ass of myself.

MICHAEL

You must have been upset or you wouldn't have said you were and that you wanted to see me—*had* to see me and had to talk to me.

ALAN

Can you forget it? Just pretend it never happened. I know *I* have. Okay?

MICHAEL

Is something wrong between you and Fran?

ALAN

Listen, I've really got to go.

MICHAEL

Why are you in New York?

ALAN

I'm dreadfully late for dinner.

MICHAEL

Whose dinner? Where are you going?

ALAN

Is this the loo?

MICHAEL

Yes.

ALAN

Excuse me.

> [*Quickly goes into the bathroom, closes the door.*
> MICHAEL *remains silent—sits on the bed, stares into
> space.*
> *Downstairs,* EMORY *pops in from the kitchen to dis-
> cover* DONALD *and* LARRY *in quiet, intimate conver-
> sation*]

EMORY

What's-going-on-in-here-oh-Mary-don't-ask!

> [*Puts a salt cellar and pepper mill on the table.*
> HANK *enters, carrying a bottle of red wine and a
> corkscrew. Looks toward* LARRY *and* DONALD. DON-
> ALD *sees him, stands up*]

DONALD

Hank, why don't you come and join us?

HANK

That's an interesting suggestion. Whose idea is that?

DONALD

Mine.

LARRY

> [*To* HANK]

He means in a conversation.

> [BERNARD *enters from the kitchen, carrying four
> wine glasses*]

EMORY
 [*To* BERNARD]
Where're the rest of the wine glasses?

BERNARD
Ahz workin' as fas' as ah can!

EMORY
They have to be told everything. Can't let 'em out of
your sight.
 [*Breezes out to the kitchen.*
 DONALD *leaves* LARRY's *side and goes to the coffee
 table, helps himself to the cracked crab.* HANK
 opens the wine, puts it on the table.
 MICHAEL *gets up from the bed and goes down the
 stairs.*
 Downstairs, HANK *crosses to* LARRY]

HANK
I thought maybe you were abiding by the agreement.

LARRY
We have no agreement.

HANK
We *did.*

LARRY
You did. I never agreed to anything!
 [DONALD *looks up to see* MICHAEL, *raises a crab
 claw toward him*]

DONALD
To your health.

MICHAEL
Up yours.

DONALD
Up my health?

BERNARD
Where's the gent?

MICHAEL
In the gent's room. If you can all hang on for five more
minutes, he's about to leave.
[*The door buzzes.* MICHAEL *crosses to it*]

LARRY
Well, at last!
[MICHAEL *opens the door to reveal a muscle-bound
young* MAN *wearing boots, tight Levi's, a calico
neckerchief, and a cowboy hat. Around his wrist
there is a large card tied with a ribbon*]

COWBOY
[*Singing fast*]
"Happy birthday to you,
Happy birthday to you,
Happy birthday, dear Harold.
Happy birthday to you."
[*And with that, he throws his arms around* MI-
CHAEL *and gives him a big kiss on the lips. Every-
one stands in stunned silence*]

MICHAEL
Who the hell are you?
[EMORY *swings in from the kitchen*]

EMORY
She's Harold's present from me and she's *early!*
[*Quick, to* COWBOY]
And that's not even Harold, you *idiot!*

COWBOY

You said whoever answered the door.

EMORY

But *not until midnight!*
  [*Quickly, to group*]
He's supposed to be a *midnight cowboy!*

DONALD

He *is* a midnight cowboy.

MICHAEL

He looks right out of a William Inge play to me.

EMORY

  [*To* COWBOY]
. . . Not until midnight and you're supposed to sing to the right person, for Chrissake! I *told* you Harold has very, very tight, tight, black curly hair.
  [*Referring to* MICHAEL]
This number's practically bald!

MICHAEL

Thank you and fuck you.

BERNARD

It's a good thing *I* didn't open the door.

EMORY

Not that tight and not that black.

COWBOY

I forgot. Besides, I wanted to get to the bars by midnight.

MICHAEL

He's a class act all the way around.

EMORY

What do you mean—get to the bars! Sweetie, I paid you for the whole night, remember?

COWBOY

I hurt my back doing my exercises and I wanted to get to bed early tonight.

BERNARD

Are you ready for this one?

LARRY

[*To* COWBOY]
That's too bad, what happened?

COWBOY

I lost my grip doing my chin-ups and I fell on my heels and twisted my back.

EMORY

You shouldn't *wear* heels when you do chin-ups.

COWBOY

[*Oblivious*]
I shouldn't do chin-ups—I got a weak grip to begin with.

EMORY

A weak grip. In my day it used to be called a limp wrist.

BERNARD

Who can remember that far back?

MICHAEL

Who was it that always used to say, "You show me Oscar Wilde in a cowboy suit, and I'll show you a gay caballero."

DONALD
I don't know. Who *was* it who always used to say that?

MICHAEL
[*Katharine Hepburn voice*]
I don't know. Somebody.

LARRY
[*To* COWBOY]
What does your card say?

COWBOY
[*Holds up his wrist*]
Here. Read it.

LARRY
[*Reading card*]
"Dear Harold, bang, bang, you're alive. But roll over and play dead. Happy birthday, Emory."

BERNARD
Ah, sheer poetry, Emmy.

LARRY
And in your usual good taste.

MICHAEL
Yes, so conservative of you to resist a sign in Times Square.

EMORY
[*Glancing toward stairs*]
Cheese it! Here comes the socialite nun.

MICHAEL
Goddammit, Emory!
[ALAN *comes down the stairs into the room. Everybody quiets*]

[85]

ALAN
Well, I'm off. . . . Thanks, Michael, for the drink.

MICHAEL
You're entirely welcome, Alan. See you tomorrow?

ALAN
. . . No. No, I think I'm going to be awfully busy. I may
even go back to Washington.

EMORY
Got a heavy date in Lafayette Square?

ALAN
What?

HANK
Emory.

EMORY
Forget it.

ALAN
    [Sees COWBOY]
Are you . . . Harold?

EMORY
No, he's not Harold. He's *for* Harold.
    [Silence. ALAN *lets it pass. Turns to* HANK]

ALAN
Goodbye, Hank. It was nice to meet you.

HANK
Same here.
    [*They shake hands*]

[86]

ALAN

If . . . if you're ever in Washington—I'd like for you to meet my wife.

LARRY

That'd be fun, wouldn't it, Hank.

EMORY

Yeah, they'd love to meet him—*her*. I have such a problem with pronouns.

ALAN
[*Quick, to* EMORY]
How many esses are there in the word pronoun?

EMORY

How'd you like to kiss my ass—that's got two or more *essessss* in it!

ALAN

How'd you like to blow me!

EMORY

What's the matter with your *wife*, she got lockjaw?

ALAN
[*Lashes out*]
Faggot, fairy, pansy . . .
[*Lunges at* EMORY]
. . . queer, cocksucker! I'll kill you, you goddamn little mincing swish! You goddamn freak! FREAK! FREAK!
[*Pandemonium.*
ALAN *beats* EMORY *to the floor before anyone recovers from surprise and reacts*]

EMORY

Oh, my God, somebody help me! Bernard! He's killing me!

[87]

[BERNARD *and* HANK *rush forward.* EMORY *is screaming. Blood gushes from his nose*]

HANK
Alan! ALAN! ALAN!

EMORY
Get him off me! Get him off me! Oh, my God, he's broken my nose! I'm BLEEDING TO DEATH!
[LARRY *has gone to shut the door.*
With one great athletic move, HANK *forcefully tears* ALAN *off* EMORY, *and drags him backward across the room.* BERNARD *bends over* EMORY, *puts his arm around him and lifts him*]

BERNARD
Somebody get some ice! And a cloth!
[LARRY *runs to the bar, grabs the bar towel and the ice bucket, rushes to put it on the floor beside* BERNARD *and* EMORY. BERNARD *quickly wraps some ice in the towel, holds it to* EMORY's *mouth*]

EMORY
Oh, my face!

BERNARD
He busted your lip, that's all. It'll be all right.
[HANK *has gotten* ALAN *down on the floor on the opposite side of the room.* ALAN *relinquishes the struggle, collapses against* HANK, *moaning and beating his fists rhythmically against* HANK's *chest.* MICHAEL *is still standing in the same spot in the center of the room, immobile.* DONALD *crosses past the* COWBOY]

DONALD
[*To* COWBOY]
Would you mind waiting over there with the gifts.
[COWBOY *moves over to where the gift-wrapped*

packages have been put. DONALD *continues past to observe the mayhem, turns up his glass, takes a long swallow.*
The door buzzes. DONALD *turns toward* MICHAEL, *waits.* MICHAEL *doesn't move.* DONALD *goes to the door, opens it to reveal* HAROLD]

Well, Harold! Happy birthday. You're just in time for the floor show, which, as you see, is on the floor.
[*To* COWBOY]
Hey, you, *this* is Harold!
[HAROLD *looks blankly toward* MICHAEL. MICHAEL *looks back blankly*]

COWBOY
[*Crossing to* HAROLD]
"Happy birthday to you,
 Happy birthday to you,
 Happy birthday, dear Harold.
 Happy birthday to you."
[*Throws his arms around* HAROLD *and gives him a big kiss.* DONALD *looks toward* MICHAEL, *who observes this stoically.* HAROLD *breaks away from* COWBOY, *reads the card, begins to laugh.*
MICHAEL *turns to survey the room.* DONALD *watches him. Slowly* MICHAEL *begins to move. Walks over to the bar, pours a glass of gin, raises it to his lips, downs it all.* DONALD *watches silently as* HAROLD *laughs and laughs and laughs*]

Curtain

Act 2

A moment later. HAROLD *is still laughing.* MICHAEL, *still at the bar, lowers his glass, turns to* HAROLD.

MICHAEL
What's so fucking funny?

HAROLD
[*Unintimidated. Quick hand to hip*]
Life. Life is a goddamn laff-riot. You remember life.

MICHAEL
You're stoned. It shows in your arm.

LARRY
Happy birthday, Harold.

MICHAEL
[*To* HAROLD]
You're stoned and you're late! You were supposed to arrive at this location at approximately eight-thirty dash nine o'clock!

HAROLD
What I *am*, Michael, is a thirty-two-year-old, ugly, pockmarked Jew fairy—and if it takes me a while to pull myself together and if I smoke a little grass before

[93]

I can get up the nerve to show this face to the world,
it's nobody's goddamn business but my own.

[*Instant switch to chatty tone*]

And how are *you* this evening?

[HANK *lifts* ALAN *to the couch.* MICHAEL *turns away
from* HAROLD, *pours himself another drink.* DONALD
watches.

HAROLD *sweeps past* MICHAEL *over to where* BER-
NARD *is helping* EMORY *up off the floor.* LARRY *returns the bucket to the bar.* MICHAEL *puts some ice
in his drink*]

EMORY

Happy birthday, Hallie.

HAROLD

What happened to *you?*

EMORY

[*Groans*]

Don't ask!

HAROLD

Your lips are turning blue; you look like you been rim-
ming a snowman.

EMORY

That piss-elegant kooze hit me!

[*Indicates* ALAN. HAROLD *looks toward the couch.*
ALAN *has slumped his head forward into his own
lap*]

MICHAEL

Careful, Emory, that kind of talk just makes him
s'nervous.

[ALAN *covers his ears with his hands*]

HAROLD
Who is she? Who was she? Who does she hope to be?

EMORY
Who knows, who cares!

HANK
His name is Alan McCarthy.

MICHAEL
Do forgive me for not formally introducing you.

HAROLD
[*Sarcastically, to* MICHAEL]
Not the famous college *chum.*

MICHAEL
[*Takes an ice cube out of his glass, throws it at*
HAROLD]
Do a figure eight on that.

HAROLD
Well, well, well. I finally get to meet dear ole Alan after all these years. And in black tie too. Is this my surprise from you, Michael?

LARRY
I think Alan is the one who got the surprise.

DONALD
And, if you'll notice, he's absolutely speechless.

EMORY
I *hope* she's in *shock!* She's a beast!

COWBOY
[*Indicating* ALAN]
Is it his birthday too?

[95]

EMORY
[*Indicates* COWBOY *to* HAROLD]
That's your surprise.

LARRY
Speaking of beasts.

EMORY
From me to you, darlin'. How do you like it?

HAROLD
Oh, I suppose he has an interesting face and body—but
it turns me right off because he can't talk intelligently
about art.

EMORY
Yeah, ain't it a shame.

HAROLD
I could never *love* anyone like that.

EMORY
Never. *Who could?*

HAROLD
I could and *you* could, that's who could! Oh, Mary,
she's *gorgeous!*

EMORY
She may be dumb, but she's all yours!

HAROLD
In affairs of the heart, there are no rules! Where'd you
ever find him?

EMORY
Rae knew where.

MICHAEL
[*To* DONALD]
Rae is Rae Clark. That's R-A-E. She's Emory's dike friend who sings at a place in the Village. She wears pin-striped suits and bills herself "Miss Rae Clark— Songs Tailored To Your Taste."

EMORY
Miss Rae Clark. Songs tailored to your taste!

MICHAEL
Have you ever heard of anything so crummy in your life?

EMORY
Rae's a fabulous chanteuse. I adore the way she does: "Down in the Depths on the Ninetieth Floor."

MICHAEL
The faggot national anthem.
[*Exits to the kitchen singing "Down in the Depths" in a butch baritone*]

HAROLD
[*To* EMORY]
All I can say is thank God for Miss Rae Clark. I think my present is a super-surprise. I'm so thrilled to get it I'd kiss you but I don't want to get blood all over me.

EMORY
Ohhh, look at my sweater!

HAROLD
Wait'll you see your face.

BERNARD
Come on, Emory, let's clean you up. Happy birthday, Harold.

HAROLD
[*Smiles*]
Thanks, love.

EMORY
My sweater is ruined!

MICHAEL
[*From the kitchen*]
Take one of mine in the bedroom.

DONALD
The one on the floor is vicuña.

BERNARD
[*To* EMORY]
You'll feel better after I bathe your face.

EMORY
Cheer-up-things-could-get-worse-I-did-and-they-did.
[BERNARD *leads* EMORY *up the stairs*]

HAROLD
Just another birthday party with the folks.
[MICHAEL *returns with a wine bottle and a green-crystal white-wine glass, pouring en route*]

MICHAEL
Here's a cold bottle of Pouilly-Fuissé I bought especially for you, kiddo.

HAROLD
Pussycat, all is forgiven. You can stay. No. You can stay,
but not all is forgiven. Cheers.

MICHAEL
I didn't want it this way, Hallie.

HAROLD
    [*Indicating* ALAN]
Who asked Mr. Right to celebrate my birthday?

DONALD
There are no accidents.

HAROLD
    [*Referring to* DONALD]
And who asked *him?*

MICHAEL
Guilty again. When I make problems for myself, I go
the whole route.

HAROLD
Always got to have your crutch, haven't you.

DONALD
I'm *not* leaving.
    [*Goes to the bar, makes himself another martini*]

HAROLD
Nobody ever thinks completely of somebody else. They
always please themselves; they always cheat, if only a
little bit.

LARRY
    [*Referring to* ALAN]
Why is he sitting there with his hands over his ears?

DONALD
I think he has an ick.
    [DONALD *looks at* MICHAEL. MICHAEL *returns the
    look, steely*]

HANK
    [*To* ALAN]

Can I get you a drink?

LARRY

How can he hear you, dummy, with his hands over his ears?

HAROLD

He can hear every word. In fact, he wouldn't miss a word if it killed him.

[ALAN *removes his hands from his ears*]

What'd I tell you?

ALAN

I . . . I . . . feel sick. I think . . . I'm going to . . . throw up.

HAROLD

Say that again and I won't have to take my appetite depressant.

[ALAN *looks desperately toward* HANK]

HANK

Hang on.

[HANK *pulls* ALAN's *arm around his neck, lifts him up, takes him up the stairs*]

HAROLD

Easy does it. One step at a time.

[BERNARD *and* EMORY *come out of the bath*]

BERNARD

There. Feel better?

EMORY

Oh, Mary, what would I do without you?

[EMORY *looks at himself in the mirror*]

I am not ready for my close-up, Mr. De Mille. Nor will I be for the next two weeks.

[BERNARD *picks up* MICHAEL's *sweater off the floor.*
HANK *and* ALAN *are midway up the stairs*]

ALAN

I'm going to throw up! Let me go! Let me go!
[*Tears loose of* HANK, *bolts up the remainder of
the stairs. He and* EMORY *meet head-on.* EMORY
screams]

EMORY

Oh, my God, he's after me again!
[EMORY *recoils as* ALAN *whizzes past him into the
bathroom, slamming the door behind him.* HANK
has reached the bedroom]

HANK

He's sick.

BERNARD

Yeah, sick in the head. Here, Emory, put this on.

EMORY

Oh, Mary, take me home. My nerves can't stand any
more of this tonight.
[EMORY *takes the vicuña sweater from* BERNARD,
starts to put it on.
Downstairs, HAROLD *flamboyantly takes out a cigarette, takes a kitchen match from a striker, steps
up on the seat of the couch and sits on the back
of it*]

HAROLD

TURNING ON!
[*With that, he strikes the match on the sole of his
shoe and lights up. Through a strained throat*]
Anybody care to join me?
[*Waves the cigarette in a slow pass*]

MICHAEL
Many thanks, no.
[HAROLD *passes it to* LARRY, *who nods negatively*]

DONALD
No, thank you.

HAROLD
[*To* COWBOY]
How about you, Tex?

COWBOY
Yeah.
[COWBOY *takes the cigarette, makes some audible inhalations through his teeth*]

MICHAEL
I find the sound of the ritual alone utterly humiliating.
[*Turns away, goes to the bar, makes another drink*]

LARRY
I hate the smell poppers leave on your fingers.

HAROLD
Why don't you get up and wash your hands?
[EMORY *and* BERNARD *come down the stairs*]

EMORY
Michael, I left the casserole in the oven. You can take it out any time.

MICHAEL
You're not going.

EMORY
I couldn't eat now anyway.

HAROLD
Well, *I'm* absolutely ravenous. I'm going to eat until I have a fat attack.

MICHAEL
[*To* EMORY]
I said, you're *not going.*

HAROLD
[*To* MICHAEL]
Having a cocktail this evening, are we? In my honor?

EMORY
It's your favorite dinner, Hallie. I made it myself.

BERNARD
Who fixed the casserole?

EMORY
Well, *I* made the sauce!

BERNARD
Well, *I* made the salad!

LARRY
Girls, please.

MICHAEL
Please *what!*

HAROLD
Beware the hostile fag. When he's sober, he's dangerous. When he drinks, he's lethal.

MICHAEL
[*Referring to* HAROLD]
Attention must *not* be paid.

HAROLD

I'm starved, Em, I'm ready for some of your Alice B.
Toklas' opium-baked lasagna.

EMORY

Are you really? Oh, that makes me so pleased maybe
I'll just serve it before I leave.

MICHAEL
You're not leaving.

BERNARD
I'll help.

LARRY

I better help too. We don't need a nose-bleed in the
lasagna.

BERNARD

When the sauce is on it, you wouldn't be able to tell
the difference anyway.
[EMORY, BERNARD, *and* LARRY *exit to the kitchen*]

MICHAEL
[*Proclamation*]
Nobody's going anywhere!

HAROLD

You are going to have schmertz tomorrow you wouldn't
believe.

MICHAEL

May I kiss the hem of your schmata, Doctor Freud?

COWBOY
What are you two talking about? I don't understand.

[104]

DONALD
He's working through his Oedipus complex, sugar.
With a machete.

COWBOY
Huh?
    [HANK *comes down the stairs*]

HANK
Michael, is there any air spray?

HAROLD
Hair spray! You're supposed to be holding his head, not
doing his hair.

HANK
Air spray, not *hair* spray.

MICHAEL
There's a can of floral spray right on top of the john.

HANK
Thanks.
    [HANK *goes back upstairs*]

HAROLD
    [*To* MICHAEL]
Aren't you going to say "If it was a snake, it would have
bitten you."

MICHAEL
    [*Indicating* COWBOY]
That is something only your friend would say.

HAROLD
    [*To* MICHAEL]
I am turning on and you are just turning.
    [*To* DONALD]

I keep my grass in the medicine cabinet. In a Band-Aid box. Somebody told me it's the safest place. If the cops arrive, you can always lock yourself in the bathroom and flush it down the john.

DONALD

Very cagey.

HAROLD

It makes more sense than where I *was* keeping it—in an oregano jar in the spice rack. I kept forgetting and accidentally turning my hateful mother on with the salad.
    [*A beat*]
But I think she liked it. No matter what meal she comes over for—even if it's breakfast—she says, "Let's have a salad!"

COWBOY

    [*To* MICHAEL]
Why do you say I would say "If it was a snake, it would have bitten you." I think that's what I *would* have said.

MICHAEL

Of course you would have, baby. That's the kind of remark your pint-size brain thinks of. You are definitely the type who still moves his lips when he reads and who sits in a steam room and says things like "Hot enough for you?"

COWBOY

I never use the steam room when I go to the gym. It's bad after a workout. It flattens you down.

MICHAEL

Just after you've broken your back to blow yourself up like a poisoned dog.

COWBOY
Yeah.

MICHAEL
You're right, Harold. Not only can he not talk intelligently about art, he can't even follow from one sentence to the next.

HAROLD
But he's beautiful. He has *unnatural* natural beauty.
[*Quick palm upheld*]
Not that that means anything.

MICHAEL
It doesn't mean *everything*.

HAROLD
Keep telling yourself that as your hair drops out in handfuls.
[*Quick palm upheld*]
Not that it's not *natural* for one's hair to recede as one reaches seniority. Not that those wonderful lines that have begun creasing our countenances don't make all the difference in the world because they add so much *character*.

MICHAEL
Faggots are worse than women about their age. They think their lives are over at thirty. Physical beauty is not that goddamned important!

HAROLD
Of course not. How could it be—it's only in the eye of the beholder.

MICHAEL
And it's only skin deep—don't forget that one.

HAROLD

Oh, no, I haven't forgotten that one at all. It's only skin deep and it's *transitory* too. It's *terribly* transitory. I mean, how long does it last—thirty or forty or fifty years at the most—depending on how well you take care of yourself. And not counting, of course, that you might die before it runs out anyway. Yes, it's too bad about this poor boy's face. It's tragic. He's absolutely cursed!

[*Takes* COWBOY's *face in his hands*]

How can *his* beauty ever compare with *my* soul? And although I have never seen my soul, I understand from my mother's rabbi that it's a knockout. I, however, cannot seem to locate it for a gander. And if I could, I'd sell it in a flash for some skin-deep, transitory, meaningless beauty!

[ALAN *walks weakly into the bedroom and sits on the bed. Downstairs,* LARRY *enters from the kitchen with salad plates.* HANK *comes into the bedroom and turns out the lamps.* ALAN *lies down. Now only the light from the bathroom and the stairwell illuminate the room*]

MICHAEL

[*Makes sign of the cross with his drink in hand*]
Forgive him, Father, for he know not what he do.

[HANK *stands still in the half darkness*]

HAROLD

Michael, you kill me. You don't know what side of the fence you're on. If somebody says something pro-religion, you're against them. If somebody denies God, you're against *them*. One might say that you have some problem in that area. You can't live with it and you can't live without it.

[EMORY *barges through the swinging door, carrying the casserole*]

EMORY
Hot stuff! Comin' through!

MICHAEL
[*To* EMORY]
One could murder you with very little effort.

HAROLD
[*To* MICHAEL]
You hang on to that great insurance policy called The Church.

MICHAEL
That's right. I believe in God, and if it turns out that there really isn't one, okay. Nothing lost. But if it turns out that there *is*—I'm covered.
[BERNARD *enters, carrying a huge salad bowl. He puts it down, lights table candles*]

EMORY
[*To* MICHAEL]
Harriet Hypocrite, that's who you are.

MICHAEL
Right. I'm one of those truly rotten Catholics who gets drunk, sins all night and goes to Mass the next morning.

EMORY
Gilda Guilt. It depends on what you think sin is.

MICHAEL
Would you just shut up your goddamn minty mouth and get back to the goddamn kitchen!

EMORY
Say anything you want—*just don't hit me!*
[*Exits. A beat*]

MICHAEL

Actually, I suppose Emory has a point—I only go to confession before I get on a plane.

BERNARD

Do you think God's power only exists at thirty thousand feet?

MICHAEL

It must. On the ground, I *am* God. In the air, I'm just one more scared son of a bitch.
[*A beat*]

BERNARD

I'm scared on the ground.

COWBOY

Me, too.
[*A beat*]
That is, when I'm not high on pot or up on acid.
[HANK *comes down the stairs*]

LARRY

[*To* HANK]
Well, is it bigger than a breadstick?

HANK

[*Ignores last remark. To* MICHAEL]
He's lying down for a minute.

HAROLD

How does the bathroom smell?

HANK

Better.

MICHAEL

Before it smelled like somebody puked. Now it smells

like somebody puked in a gardenia patch.

LARRY
And how does the big hero feel?

HANK
Lay off, will you.
[EMORY *enters with a basket of napkin-covered rolls, deposits them on the table*]

EMORY
Dinner is served!
[HAROLD *comes to the buffet table*]

HAROLD
Emory, it looks absolutely fabulous.

EMORY
I'd make somebody a good wife.
[EMORY *serves pasta.* BERNARD *serves the salad, pours wine.* MICHAEL *goes to the bar, makes another drink*]
I could cook and do an apartment and entertain . . .
[*Grabs a long-stem rose from an arrangement on the table, clenches it between his teeth, snaps his fingers and strikes a pose*]
Kiss me quick, I'm Carmen!
[HAROLD *just looks at him blankly, passes on.* EMORY *takes the flower out of his mouth*]
One really needs castanets for that sort of thing.

MICHAEL
And a getaway car.
[HANK *comes up to the table*]

EMORY
What would you like, big boy?

LARRY
Alan McCarthy, and don't hold the mayo.

EMORY
I can't keep up with you two—
[*Indicating* HANK, *then* LARRY]
—I thought you were mad at him—now he's bitchin'
you. What gives?

LARRY
Never mind.
[COWBOY *comes over to the table.* EMORY *gives him
a plate of food.* BERNARD *gives him salad and a
glass of wine.*
HANK *moves to the couch, sits and puts his plate
and glass on the coffee table.*
HAROLD *moves to sit on the stairs and eat*]

COWBOY
What is it?

LARRY
Lasagna.

COWBOY
It looks like spaghetti and meatballs sorta flattened out.

DONALD
It's been in the steam room.

COWBOY
It has?

MICHAEL
[*Contemptuously*]
It looks like spaghetti and meatballs sorta flattened out.
Ah, yes, Harold, truly enviable.

HAROLD

As opposed to you who knows so much about *haute cuisine*.
> [*A beat*]

Raconteur, gourmet, troll.
> [LARRY *takes a plate of food, goes to sit on the back of the couch from behind it*]

COWBOY

It's good.

HAROLD
> [*Quick*]

You like it, eat it.

MICHAEL

Stuff your mouth so that you can't say anything.
> [DONALD *takes a plate*]

HAROLD

Turning.

BERNARD
> [*To* DONALD]

Wine?

DONALD

No, thanks.

MICHAEL

Aw, go on, kiddo, force yourself. Have a little *vin ordinaire* to wash down all that depressed pasta.

HAROLD

Sommelier, connoisseur, pig.
> [DONALD *takes the glass of wine, moves up by the bar, puts the glass of wine on it, leans against the wall, eats his food.* EMORY *hands* BERNARD *a plate*]

BERNARD
[*To* EMORY]
Aren't you going to have any?

EMORY
No. My lip hurts too much to eat.

MICHAEL
[*Crosses to table, picks up knife*]
I hear if you puts a knife under de bed it cuts de pain.

HAROLD
[*To* MICHAEL]
I hear if you put a knife under your chin it cuts your throat.

EMORY
Anybody going to take a plate up to Alan?

MICHAEL
The punching bag has now dissolved into Flo Nightingale.

LARRY
Hank?

HANK
I don't think he'd have any appetite.
[ALAN, *as if he's heard his name, gets up from the bed, moves slowly to the top of the stairwell.* BERNARD *takes his plate, moves near the stairs, sits on the floor.* MICHAEL *raps the knife on an empty wine glass*]

MICHAEL
Ladies and gentlemen. Correction: Ladies and ladies, I would like to announce that you have just eaten Sebastian Venable.

COWBOY
Just eaten *what?*

MICHAEL
Not *what*, stupid. *Who*. A character in a play. A fairy who was eaten alive. I mean the chop-chop variety.

COWBOY
Jesus.

HANK
Did Edward Albee write that play?

MICHAEL
No. Tennessee Williams.

HANK
Oh, yeah.

MICHAEL
Albee wrote *Who's Afraid of Virginta Woolf?*

LARRY
Dummy.

HANK
I know that. I just thought maybe he wrote that other one too.

LARRY
Well, you made a mistake.

HANK
So I made a mistake.

LARRY
That's right, you made a mistake.

HANK
What's the difference! You can't add.

COWBOY
Edward who.

MICHAEL
    [*To* EMORY]
How much did you pay for him?

EMORY
He was a steal.

MICHAEL
He's a ham sandwich—fifty cents any time of the day or night.

HAROLD
King of the Pig People.
    [MICHAEL *gives him a look.* DONALD *returns his plate to the table*]

EMORY
    [*To* DONALD]
Would you like some more?

DONALD
No, thank you, Emory. It was very good.

EMORY
Did you like it?

COWBOY
I'm not a steal. I cost twenty dollars.
    [BERNARD *returns his plate*]

EMORY
More?

BERNARD
[*Nods negatively*]
It was delicious—even if I did make it myself.

EMORY
Isn't anybody having seconds?

HAROLD
I'm having seconds and thirds and maybe even fifths.
[*Gets up off the stairs, comes toward the table*]
I'm absolutely desperate to keep the weight up.
[BERNARD *bends to whisper something in* EMORY'S *ear.* EMORY *nods affirmatively and* BERNARD *crosses to* COWBOY *and whispers in his ear. A beat.* COWBOY *returns his plate to the buffet and follows* EMORY *and* BERNARD *into the kitchen*]

MICHAEL
[*Parodying* HAROLD]
You're *absolutely* paranoid about *absolutely* every-
thing.

HAROLD
Oh, yeah, well, why don't you *not* tell me about it.

MICHAEL
You starve yourself all day, living on coffee and cottage
cheese so that you can gorge yourself at one meal. Then
you feel guilty and moan and groan about how fat you
are and how ugly you are when the truth is you're no
fatter or thinner than you ever are.

EMORY
Polly Paranoia.
[EMORY *moves to the coffee table to take* HANK'S
empty plate]

[117]

HANK
Just great, Emory.

EMORY
Connie Casserole, no-trouble-at-all-oh-Mary, D.A.

MICHAEL
[*To* HAROLD]
... And this pathological lateness. It's downright *crazy*.

HAROLD
Turning.

MICHAEL
Standing before a bathroom mirror for hours and hours
before you can walk out on the street. And looking no
different after Christ knows how many applications of
Christ knows how many ointments and salves and
creams and masks.

HAROLD
I've got bad skin, what can I tell you.

MICHAEL
Who wouldn't after they deliberately take a pair of
tweezers and *deliberately* mutilate their pores—no
wonder you've got holes in your face after the hack job
you've done on yourself year in and year out!

HAROLD
[*Coolly but definitely*]
You hateful sow.

MICHAEL
Yes, you've got scars on your face—but they're not that
bad and if you'd leave yourself alone you wouldn't have
any more than you've already awarded yourself.

HAROLD

You'd really like me to compliment you now for being so honest, wouldn't you. For being my best friend who will tell me what even my best friends won't tell me. Swine.

MICHAEL

And the pills!

[*Announcement to group*]

Harold has been gathering, saving, and storing up barbiturates for the last year like a goddamn squirrel. Hundreds of Nembutals, hundreds of Seconals. All in preparation for and anticipation of the long winter of his death.

[*Silence*]

But I tell you right now, Hallie. When the time comes, you'll never have the guts. It's not always like it happens in plays, not all faggots bump themselves off at the end of the story.

HAROLD

What you say may be true. Time will undoubtedly tell. But, in the meantime, you've left out one detail—the cosmetics and astringents are *paid* for, the bathroom is *paid* for, the tweezers are *paid* for, and the pills *are paid for!*

[EMORY *darts in and over to the light switch, plunges the room into darkness except for the light from the tapers on the buffet table, and begins to sing "Happy Birthday." Immediately* BERNARD *pushes the swinging door open and* COWBOY *enters carrying a cake ablaze with candles. Everybody has now joined in with "Happy birthday, dear Harold, happy birthday to you." This is followed by a round of applause.*

MICHAEL *turns, goes to the bar, makes another drink*]

EMORY
Blow out your candles, Mary, and make a wish!

MICHAEL
  [*To himself*]
Blow out your candles, *Laura*.
  [COWBOY *has brought cake over in front of* HAROLD.
  *He thinks a minute, blows out the candles. More
  applause*]

EMORY
Awwww, she's thirty-two years young!

HAROLD
  [*Groans, holds his head*]
Ohh, my God!
  [BERNARD *has brought in cake plates and forks. The
  room remains lit only by candlelight from the buf-
  fet table.* COWBOY *returns the cake to the table and*
  BERNARD *begins to cut it and put the pieces on the
  plates*]

HANK
Now you have to open your gifts.

HAROLD
Do I have to open them here?

EMORY
Of course you've got to open them here.
  [*Hands* HAROLD *a gift.* HAROLD *begins to rip the
  paper off*]

HAROLD
Where's the card?

EMORY
Here.

HAROLD

Oh. From Larry.
[*Finishes tearing off the paper*]
It's *heaven!* Oh, I just love it, Larry.
[HAROLD *holds up a graphic design—a large-scale deed to Boardwalk, like those used in a Monopoly game*]

COWBOY

What is it?

HAROLD

It's the deed to Boardwalk.

EMORY

Oh, gay pop art!

DONALD
[*To* LARRY]
It's sensational. Did you do it?

LARRY

Yes.

HAROLD

Oh, it's super, Larry. It goes up the minute I get home.
[HAROLD *gives* LARRY *a peck on the cheek*]

COWBOY
[*To* HAROLD]
I don't get it—you cruise Atlantic City or something?

MICHAEL

Will somebody get him out of here!
[HAROLD *has torn open another gift, takes the card from inside*]

HAROLD

Oh, what a nifty sweater! Thank you, Hank.

HANK

You can take it back and pick out another one if you
want to.

HAROLD

I think this one is just nifty.
   [DONALD *goes to the bar, makes himself a brandy*
   and soda]

BERNARD

Who wants cake?

EMORY

Everybody?

DONALD

None for me.

MICHAEL

I'd just like to sleep on mine, thank you.
   [HANK *comes over to the table.* BERNARD *gives him*
   a plate of cake, passes another one to COWBOY *and*
   a third to LARRY. HAROLD *has torn the paper off an-*
   other gift. Suddenly laughs aloud]

HAROLD

Oh, Bernard! How divine! Look, everybody! Bejeweled
knee pads!
   [*Holds up a pair of basketball knee pads with*
   sequin initials]

BERNARD

Monogrammed!

EMORY
Bernard, you're a camp!

MICHAEL
Y'all heard of Gloria DeHaven and Billy de Wolfe, well, dis here is Rosemary De Camp!

BERNARD
Who?

EMORY
I never miss a Rosemary De Camp picture.

HANK
I've never heard of her.

COWBOY
Me neither.

HANK
Not all of us spent their childhood in a movie house, Michael. Some of us played baseball.

DONALD
And mowed the lawn.

EMORY
Well, *I* know who Rosemary De Camp is.

MICHAEL
You would. It's a cinch you wouldn't recognize a baseball or a lawnmower.
[HAROLD *has unwrapped his last gift. He is silent. Pause*]

HAROLD
Thank you, Michael.

[123]

MICHAEL
What?
    [*Turns to see the gift*]
Oh.
    [*A beat*]
You're welcome.
    [MICHAEL *finishes off his drink, returns to the bar*]

LARRY
What is it, Harold?
    [*A beat*]

HAROLD
It's a photograph of him in a silver frame. And there's
an inscription engraved and the date.

BERNARD
What's it say?

HAROLD
Just . . . something personal.
    [MICHAEL *spins round from the bar*]

MICHAEL
Hey, Bernard, what do you say we have a little music
to liven things up!

BERNARD
Okay.

EMORY
Yeah, I feel like dancing.

MICHAEL
How about something good and ethnic, Emory—one of
your specialties, like a military toe tap with sparklers.

EMORY

I don't do that at birthdays—only on the Fourth of July.
[BERNARD *puts on a romantic record.* EMORY *goes
to* BERNARD. *They start to dance slowly*]

LARRY

Come on, Michael.

MICHAEL

I only lead.

LARRY

I can follow.
[*They start to dance*]

HAROLD

Come on, Tex, you're on.
[COWBOY *gets to his feet, but is a washout as a
dancing partner.* HAROLD *gives up, takes out another cigarette, strikes a match. As he does, he catches
sight of someone over by the stairs, walks over to*
ALAN. *Blows out match*]
Wanna dance?

EMORY

[*Sees* ALAN]
Uh-oh. Yvonne the Terrible is back.

MICHAEL

Oh, hello, Alan. Feel better? This is where you came
in, isn't it?
[ALAN *starts to cross directly to the door.* MICHAEL
breaks away]
Excuse me, Larry . . .
[ALAN *has reached the door and has started to open
it as* MICHAEL *intercepts, slams the door with one
hand, and leans against it, crossing his legs*]

As they say in the Deep South, don't rush off in the heat of the day.

HAROLD

Revolution complete.

> [MICHAEL *slowly takes* ALAN *by the arm, walks him slowly back into the room*]

MICHAEL

. . . You missed the cake—and you missed the opening of the gifts—but you're still in luck. You're just in time for a party game.

> [*They have reached the phonograph.* MICHAEL *rejects the record. The music stops, the dancing stops.* MICHAEL *releases* ALAN, *claps his hands*]

. . . Hey, everybody! Game time!

> [ALAN *starts to move.* MICHAEL *catches him gently by the sleeve*]

HAROLD

Why don't you just let him go, Michael?

MICHAEL

He can go if he wants to—but not before we play a little game.

EMORY

What's it going to be—movie-star gin?

MICHAEL

That's too faggy for Alan to play—he wouldn't be any good at it.

BERNARD

What about Likes and Dislikes?

> [MICHAEL *lets go of* ALAN, *takes a pencil and pad from the desk*]

MICHAEL

It's too much trouble to find enough pencils, and besides, Emory always puts down the same thing. He dislikes artificial fruit and flowers and coffee grinders made into lamps—and he likes Mabel Mercer, poodles, and *All About Eve*—the screenplay of which he will then recite *verbatim*.

EMORY

I put down other things sometimes.

MICHAEL

Like a tan out of season?

EMORY

I just always put down little "Chi-Chi" because I adore her so much.

MICHAEL

If one is of the masculine gender, a poodle is the *insignia* of one's deviation.

BERNARD

You know why old ladies like poodles—because they go down on them.

EMORY·

They do not!

LARRY

We could play B for Botticelli.

MICHAEL

We *could* play *Spin* the Botticelli, but we're not going to.

[*A beat*]

HAROLD

What would you like to play, Michael—the Truth Game?

[MICHAEL *chuckles to himself*]

MICHAEL

Cute, Hallie.

HAROLD

Or do you want to play Murder? You all remember that one, don't you?

MICHAEL

[*To* HAROLD]
Very, very cute.

DONALD

As I recall, they're quite similar. The rules are the same in both—you kill somebody.

MICHAEL

In affairs of the heart, there are no rules. Isn't that right, Harold?

HAROLD

That's what I always say.

MICHAEL

Well, that's the name of the game. The Affairs of the Heart.

COWBOY

I've never heard of that one.

MICHAEL

Of course you've never heard of it—I just made it up, baby doll. Affairs of the Heart is a combination of both the Truth Game and Murder—with a new twist.

HAROLD
I can hardly wait to find out what that is.

ALAN
Mickey, I'm leaving.
   [*Starts to move*]

MICHAEL
   [*Firmly, flatly*]
Stay where you are.

HAROLD
Michael, let him go.

MICHAEL
He really doesn't *want* to. If he did, he'd have left a long time ago—or he wouldn't have come here in the first place.

ALAN
   [*Holding his forehead*]
... Mickey, I don't *feel* well!

MICHAEL
   [*Low tone, but distinctly articulate*]
My name is Michael. I am called Michael. You must never call anyone called Michael Mickey. Those of us who are named Michael are very nervous about it. If you don't believe it—try it.

ALAN
I'm sorry. I can't think.

MICHAEL
You can think. What you can't do—is leave. It's like watching an accident on the highway—you can't look at it and you can't look away.

ALAN
I ... feel ... weak ...

MICHAEL
You are weak. Much weaker than I think you realize.
    [*Takes* ALAN *by the arm, leads him to a chair.
    Slowly, deliberately, pushes him down into it*]
Now! Who's going to play with Alan and me? Every-
one?

HAROLD
I have no intention of playing.

DONALD
Nor do I.

MICHAEL
Well, not everyone is a participant in *life*. There are
always those who stand on the sidelines and watch.

LARRY
What's the game?

MICHAEL
Simply this: we all have to call on the telephone the
one person we truly believe we have loved.

HANK
I'm not playing.

LARRY
Oh, yes, you are.

HANK
You'd like for me to play, wouldn't you?

LARRY
You bet I would. I like to know who you'd call after all

the fancy speeches I've heard lately. Who would you call? Would you call me?

MICHAEL
[*To* BERNARD]
Sounds like there's, how you say, trouble in paradise.

HAROLD
If there isn't, I think you'll be able to stir up some.

HANK
And who would *you* call? Don't think I think for one minute it would be me. Or that one call would do it. You'd have to make several, wouldn't you? About three long-distance and God only knows how many locals.

COWBOY
I'm glad I don't have to pay the bill.

MICHAEL
Quiet!

HAROLD
[*Loud whisper to* COWBOY]
Oh, don't worry, Michael won't pay it either.

MICHAEL
Now, here's how it works.

LARRY
I thought you said there were no rules.

MICHAEL
That's right. In Affairs of the Heart, there are no rules! This is the goddamn point system!
[*No response from anyone. A beat*]
If you make the call, you get one point. If the person you are calling answers, you get two more points. If

somebody else answers, you get only one. If there's no answer at all, you're screwed.

DONALD
You're screwed if you make the call.

HAROLD
You're a *fool*—if you screw yourself.

MICHAEL
... When you get the person whom you are calling on the line—if you tell them who you are, you get two points. And then—if you tell them that you *love* them—you get a bonus of five more points!

HAROLD
Hateful.

MICHAEL
Therefore you can get as many as ten points and as few as one.

HAROLD
You can get as few as none—if you know how to work it.

MICHAEL
The one with the highest score wins.

ALAN
Hank. Let's get out of here.

EMORY
Well, now. Did you hear that!

MICHAEL
Just the two of you together. The pals ... the guys ... the buddy-buddies ... the he-men.

EMORY
I think Larry might have something to say about that.

BERNARD
Emory.

MICHAEL
The duenna speaks.
[*Crosses to take the telephone from the desk, brings it to the group*]
So who's playing? Not including Cowboy, who, as a gift, is neuter. And, of course, le voyeur.
[*A beat*]
Emory? Bernard?

BERNARD
I don't think I want to play.

MICHAEL
Why, Bernard! Where's your fun-loving spirit?

BERNARD
I don't think this game is fun.

HAROLD
It's absolutely hateful.

ALAN
Hank, leave with me.

HANK
You don't understand, Alan. I can't. You can . . . but I can't.

ALAN
Why, Hank? Why can't you?

LARRY
[*To* HANK]
If he doesn't understand, why don't you explain it to him?

MICHAEL
I'll explain it.

HAROLD
I had a feeling you might.

MICHAEL
Although I doubt that it'll make any difference. That type refuses to understand that which they do not wish to accept. They reject certain facts. And Alan is decidedly from The Ostrich School of Reality.
[*A beat*]
Alan . . . Larry and Hank are lovers. Not just roommates, *bed*mates. *Lovers.*

ALAN
Michael!

MICHAEL
No man's still got a *roommate* when he's over thirty years old. If they're not lovers, they're sisters.

LARRY
Hank is the one who's over thirty.

MICHAEL
Well, you're pushing it!

ALAN
. . . Hank?
[*A beat*]

HANK
Yes, Alan. Larry is my lover.

ALAN
But . . . but . . . you're married.
> [MICHAEL, LARRY, EMORY, *and* COWBOY *are sent into instant gales of laughter*]

HAROLD
I think you said the wrong thing.

MICHAEL
Don't you love that quaint little idea—if a man is married, then he is automatically heterosexual.
> [*A beat*]

Alan—Hank swings both ways—with a definite preference.
> [*A beat*]

Now. Who makes the first call? Emory?

EMORY
You go, Bernard.

BERNARD
I don't want to.

EMORY
I don't want to either. I don't want to at all.

DONALD
> [*To himself*]

There are no accidents.

MICHAEL
Then, may I say, on your way home I hope you *will* yourself over an embankment.

EMORY

[*To* BERNARD]

Go on. Call up Peter Dahlbeck. That's who you'd like to call, isn't it?

MICHAEL

Who is Peter Dahlbeck?

EMORY

The boy in Detroit whose family Bernard's mother has been a laundress for since he was a pickaninny.

BERNARD

I worked for them too—after school and every summer.

EMORY

It's always been a large order of Hero Worship.

BERNARD

I think I've loved him all my life. But he never knew I was alive. Besides, he's straight.

COWBOY

So nothing ever happened between you?

EMORY

Oh, they finally made it—in the pool house one night after a drunken swimming party.

LARRY

With the right wine and the right music there're damn few that aren't curious.

MICHAEL

Sounds like there's a lot of Lady Chatterley in Mr. Dahlbeck, wouldn't you say, Donald?

DONALD

I've never been an O'Hara fan myself.

[136]

BERNARD
. . . And afterwards we went swimming in the nude in the dark with only the moon reflecting on the water.

DONALD
Nor Thomas Merton.

BERNARD
It was beautiful.

MICHAEL
How romantic. And then the next morning you took him his coffee and Alka-Seltzer on a tray.

BERNARD
It was in the afternoon. I remember I was worried sick all morning about having to face him. But he pretended like nothing at all had happened.

MICHAEL
Christ, he must have been so drunk he didn't remember a thing.

BERNARD
Yeah. I was sure relieved.

MICHAEL
Odd how that works. And now, for ten points, get that liar on the phone.
    [*A beat.* BERNARD *picks up the phone, dials*]

LARRY
You *know* the number?

BERNARD
Sure. He's back in Grosse Pointe, living at home. He just got separated from his third wife.
    [*All watch* BERNARD *as he puts the receiver to his ear, waits. A beat. He hangs up quickly*]

EMORY

D.A. or B.Y.?

MICHAEL

He didn't even give it time to find out.
[*Coaxing*]
Go ahead, Bernard. Pick up the phone and dial. You'll
think of something. You know you want to call him.
You know that, don't you? Well, go ahead. Your curi-
osity has got the best of you now. So ... go on, call him.
[*A beat.* BERNARD *picks up the receiver, dials again.
Lets it ring this time*]

HAROLD

Hateful.

COWBOY

What's D.A. or B.Y.?

EMORY

That's operator lingo. It means—"Doesn't Answer" or
"Busy."

BERNARD

... Hello?

MICHAEL

One point.
[*Efficiently takes note on the pad*]

BERNARD

Who's speaking? Oh ... Mrs. Dahlbeck.

MICHAEL

[*Taking note*]
One point.

BERNARD

... It's Bernard—Francine's boy.

EMORY

Son, not *boy.*

BERNARD

... How are you? Good. Good. Oh, just fine, thank you. Mrs. Dahlbeck ... is ... Peter ... at home? Oh. Oh, I see.

MICHAEL
    [*Shakes his head*]
Shhhhiiii ...

BERNARD

... Oh, no. No, it's nothing important. I just wanted to ... to tell him ... that ... to tell him I ... I ...

MICHAEL
    [*Prompting flatly*]
I love him. That I've always loved him.

BERNARD

... that I was sorry to hear about him and his wife.

MICHAEL

No points!

BERNARD

... My mother wrote me. Yes. It is. It really is. Well. Would you just tell him I called and said ... that I was ... just ... very, very sorry to hear and I ... hope ... they can get everything straightened out. Yes. Yes. Well, good night. Goodbye.
    [*Hangs up slowly.* MICHAEL *draws a definite line across his pad, makes a definite period*]

MICHAEL

Two points total. Terrible. Next!
    [MICHAEL *whisks the phone out of* BERNARD's *hands, gives it to* EMORY]

[139]

EMORY

Are you all right, Bernard?

BERNARD
  [*Almost to himself*]
Why did I call? Why did I do that?

LARRY
  [*To* BERNARD]
Where was he?

BERNARD

Out on a date.

MICHAEL

Come on, Emory. Punch in.
  [EMORY *picks up the phone, dials information. A
  beat*]

EMORY

Could I have the number, please—in the Bronx—for a
Delbert Botts.

LARRY

A Delbert Botts! How many can there be!

BERNARD

Oh, I wish I hadn't called now.

EMORY

. . . No, the residence number, please.
  [*Waves his hand at* MICHAEL, *signaling for the
  pencil.* MICHAEL *hands it to him. He writes on the
  white, plastic phone case*]
. . . Thank you.
  [*A beat. And he indignantly slams down the re-
  ceiver*]
I do wish information would stop calling me "Ma'am"!

MICHAEL
By all means, scribble all over the telephone.
  [*Snatches the pencil from* EMORY's *hands*]

EMORY
It comes off with a little spit.

MICHAEL
Like a lot of things.

LARRY
Who the hell is Delbert Botts?

EMORY
The one person I have always loved.
  [*To* MICHAEL]
That's who you said call, isn't it?

MICHAEL
That's right, Emory board.

LARRY
How could you love anybody with a name like that?

MICHAEL
Yes, Emory, you couldn't love anybody with a name
like that. It wouldn't look good on a place card. Isn't
that right. Alan?
  [MICHAEL *slaps* ALAN *on the shoulder.* ALAN *is silent.* MICHAEL *snickers*]

EMORY
I admit his name is not so good—but he is absolutely
beautiful. At least, he was when I was in high school.
Of course, I haven't seen him since and he was about
seven years older than I even then.

MICHAEL

Christ, you better call him quick before he dies.

EMORY

I've loved him ever since the first day I laid eyes on him, which was when I was in the fifth grade and he was a senior. Then, he went away to college and by the time he got out *I* was in high school, and he had become a dentist.

MICHAEL

[*With incredulous disgust*]
A dentist!

EMORY

Yes. Delbert Botts, D.D.S. And he opened his office in a bank building.

HAROLD

And you went and had every tooth in your head pulled out, right?

EMORY

No. I just had my teeth cleaned, that's all.
[DONALD *turns from the bar with two drinks in his hands*]

BERNARD

[*To himself*]
Oh, I shouldn't have called.

MICHAEL

Will you shut up, Bernard! And take your boring, sleep-making icks somewhere else. *Go!*
[MICHAEL *extends a pointed finger toward the steps.* BERNARD *takes the wine bottle and his glass and moves toward the stairs, pouring himself another drink on the way*]

EMORY

I remember I looked right into his eyes the whole time
and I kept wanting to bite his fingers.

HAROLD

Well, it's absolutely mind boggling.

MICHAEL

Phyllis Phallic.

HAROLD

It absolutely boggles the mind.
[DONALD *brings one of the drinks to* ALAN. ALAN
takes it, drinks it down]

MICHAEL
[*Referring to* DONALD]
Sara Samaritan.

EMORY

. . . I told him I was having my teeth cleaned for the
Junior-Senior Prom, for which I was in charge of deco-
rations. I told him it was a celestial theme and I was
cutting stars out of tin foil and making clouds out of
chicken wire and angel's-hair.
[*A beat*]
He couldn't have been less impressed.

COWBOY

I got angel's-hair down my shirt once at Christmas
time. Gosh, did it itch!

EMORY

. . . I told him I was going to burn incense in pots so
that white fog would hover over the dance floor and
it would look like heaven—just like I'd seen it in a Rita
Hayworth movie. I can't remember the title.

MICHAEL

The picture was called *Down to Earth*. Any *kid* knows that.

COWBOY

... And it made little tiny cuts in the creases of my fingers. Man, did they sting! It would be terrible if you got that stuff in your ...
  [MICHAEL *circles slowly toward him*]
I'll be quiet.

EMORY

He was engaged to this stupid-ass girl named Loraine whose mother was truly Supercunt.

MICHAEL

Don't digress.

EMORY

Well, anyway, I was a wreck. I mean a total mess. I couldn't eat, sleep, stand up, sit down, *nothing*. I could hardly cut out silver stars or finish the clouds for the prom. So I called him on the telephone and asked if I could see him alone.

HAROLD

Clearly not the coolest of moves.
  [DONALD *looks at* ALAN. ALAN *looks away*]

EMORY

He said okay and told me to come by his house. I was so nervous my hands were shaking and my voice was unsteady. I couldn't look at him this time—I just stared straight in space and blurted out why I'd come. I told him ... I wanted him to be my friend. I said that I had never had a friend who I could talk to and tell everything and trust. I asked him if he would be my friend.

COWBOY
You poor bastard.

MICHAEL
Shhhhhh!

BERNARD
What'd he say?

EMORY
He said he would be glad to be my friend. And any time I ever wanted to see him or call him—to just call him and he'd see me. And he shook my trembling wet hand and I left on a cloud.

MICHAEL
One of the ones you made yourself.

EMORY
And the next day I went and bought him a gold-plated cigarette lighter and had his initials monogrammed on it and wrote a card that said "From your friend, Emory."

HAROLD
Seventeen years old and already big with the gifts.

COWBOY
Yeah. And cards too.

EMORY
. . . And then the night of the prom I found out.

BERNARD
Found out what?

EMORY
I heard two girls I knew giggling together. They were

standing behind some goddamn corrugated cardboard Greek columns I had borrowed from a department store and had draped with yards and yards of goddamn cheesecloth. Oh, Mary, it takes a fairy to make something pretty.

MICHAEL
Don't digress.

EMORY
This girl who was telling the story said she had heard it from her mother—and her mother had heard it from Loraine's mother.
[*To* MICHAEL]
You see, Loraine and her mother were not beside the point.
[*Back to the group*]
Obviously, Del had told Loraine about my calling and about the gift.
[*A beat*]
Pretty soon everybody at the dance had heard about it and they were laughing and making jokes. Everybody knew I had a crush on Doctor Delbert Botts and that I had asked him to be my friend.
[*A beat*]
What they didn't know was that I *loved* him. And that I would go on loving him years after they had all forgotten my funny secret.
[*Pause*]

HAROLD
Well, I for one need an insulin injection.

MICHAEL
Call him.

BERNARD
Don't, Emory.

MICHAEL
Since when are you telling him what to do!

EMORY
[*To* BERNARD]
What do I care—I'm pissed! I'll do anything. Three times.

BERNARD
Don't. *Please!*

MICHAEL
I said call him.

BERNARD
Don't! You'll be sorry. Take my word for it.

EMORY
What have I got to lose?

BERNARD
Your dignity. That's what you've got to lose.

MICHAEL
Well, *that's* a knee-slapper! I love *your* telling *him* about dignity when you allow him to degrade you constantly by Uncle Tom-ing you to death.

BERNARD
He can do it, Michael. *I* can do it. But *you can't* do it.

MICHAEL
Isn't that discrimination?

BERNARD
I don't like it from him and I don't like it from me—but I do it to myself and I let him do it. I let him do it because it's the only thing that, to him, makes him my

equal. We both got the short end of the stick—but I got a hell of a lot more than he did and he knows it. I let him Uncle Tom me just so he can tell himself he's not a complete loser.

MICHAEL
How very considerate.

BERNARD
It's his defense. You have your defense, Michael. But it's indescribable.
[EMORY *quietly licks his finger and begins to rub the number off the telephone case*]

MICHAEL
[*To* BERNARD]
Y'all want to hear a little polite parlor jest from the liberal Deep South? Do you know why *Nigras* have such big lips? Because they're always going "P-p-p-p-a-a-a-h!"
[*The labial noise is exasperating with lazy disgust as he shuffles about the room*]

DONALD
Christ, Michael!

MICHAEL
[*Unsuccessfully tries to tear the phone away from* EMORY]
I can do without your goddamn spit all over my telephone, you nellie coward.

EMORY
I may be nellie, but I'm no coward.
[*Starts to dial*]
Bernard, forgive me. I'm sorry. I won't ever say those things to you again.

[148]

[MICHAEL *watches triumphant.* BERNARD *pours another glass of wine. A beat*]

B.Y.

MICHAEL

It's busy?

EMORY
[*Nods*]
Loraine is probably talking to her mother. Oh, yes,
Delbert married Loraine.

MICHAEL

I'm sorry, you'll have to forfeit your turn. We can't
wait.
[*Takes the phone, hands it to* LARRY, *who starts to
dial*]

HAROLD
[*To* LARRY]
Well, you're not wasting any time.

HANK

Who are you calling?

LARRY

Charlie.
[EMORY *gets up, jerks the phone out of* LARRY's
hands]

EMORY

I refuse to forfeit my turn! It's *my turn* and I'm taking
it!

MICHAEL

That's the spirit, Emory! *Hit that iceberg—don't miss
it! Hit it! Goddamnit!* I want a smash of a finale!

EMORY
Oh, God, I'm drunk.

MICHAEL
A falling-down-drunk-nellie-queen.

HAROLD
Well, that's the pot calling the kettle beige!

MICHAEL
[*Snapping. To* HAROLD]
I am not drunk! You cannot tell that I am drunk! Donald! I'm not drunk! Am I!

DONALD
I'm drunk.

EMORY
So am I. I am a *major drunk.*

MICHAEL
[*To* EMORY]
Shut up and dial!

EMORY
[*Dialing*]
I am a major drunk of this or any other season.

DONALD
[*To* MICHAEL]
Don't you mean shut up and *deal.*

EMORY
... It's ringing. It is no longer B.Y. Hello?

MICHAEL
[*Taking note*]

EMORY
. . . Who's speaking? Who? . . . Doctor Delbert Botts?

MICHAEL
Two points.

EMORY
Oh, Del, is this really you? Oh, nobody. You don't know me. You wouldn't remember me. I'm . . . just a friend. A falling-down drunken friend. Hello? Hello? Hello?
     [*Lowers the receiver*]
He hung up.
     [EMORY *hangs up the telephone*]

MICHAEL
Three points total. You're winning.

EMORY
He said I must have the wrong party.
     [BERNARD *gets up, goes into the kitchen*]

HAROLD
He's right. We have the wrong party. We should be somewhere else.

EMORY
It's your party, Hallie. Aren't you having a good time?

HAROLD
Simply fabulous. And what about you? Are you having a good time, Emory? Are you having as good a time as you thought you would?
     [LARRY *takes the phone*]

MICHAEL
If you're bored, Harold, we could sing Happy Birthday again—to the tune of Havah Nageelah.

[HAROLD *takes out another cigarette*]

HAROLD
Not for all the tea in Mexico.
[*Lights up*]

HANK
My turn now.

LARRY
It's my turn to call Charlie.

HANK
No. Let me.

LARRY
Are *you* going to call Charlie?

MICHAEL
The score is three to two. Emory's favor.

ALAN
Don't, Hank. Don't you see—Bernard was right.

HANK
[*Firmly, to* ALAN]
I want to.
[*A beat. Holds out his hand for the phone*]
Larry?
[*A beat*]

LARRY
[*Gives him the phone*]
Be my eager guest.

COWBOY
[*To* LARRY]
Is he going to call Charlie for you?

[LARRY *breaks into laughter.* HANK *starts to dial*]

LARRY
Charlie is all the people I cheat on Hank with.

DONALD
With whom I cheat on Hank.

MICHAEL
The butcher, the baker, the candlestick maker.

LARRY
Right! I love 'em all. And what he refuses to understand—is that I've got to *have* 'em all. I am *not* the mar-
rying kind, and I never will be.

HAROLD
Gypsy feet.

LARRY
Who are you calling?

MICHAEL
Jealous?

LARRY
Curious as hell!

MICHAEL
And a little jealous too.

LARRY
Who are you calling?

MICHAEL
Did it ever occur to you that Hank might be doing the
same thing behind your back that you do behind his?

LARRY

I wish to Christ he would. It'd make life a hell of a lot easier. Who are you calling?

HAROLD

Whoever it is, they're not sitting on top of the telephone.

HANK

Hello?

COWBOY

They must have been in the tub.

MICHAEL
[*Snaps at* COWBOY]
Eighty-six!
[COWBOY *goes over to a far corner, sits down.* BERNARD *enters, uncorking another bottle of wine. Taking note*]
One point.

HANK

. . . I'd like to leave a message.

MICHAEL

Not in. One point.

HANK

Would you say that Hank called. Yes, it is. Oh, good evening, how are you?

LARRY

Who the hell *is* that?

HANK

. . . Yes, that's right—the message is for my roommate, Larry. Just say that I called and . . .

LARRY
It's our answering service!

HANK
. . . and said . . . I love you.

MICHAEL
Five points! You said it! You get five goddamn points
for saying it!

ALAN
Hank! Hank! . . . Are you crazy?

HANK
. . . No. You didn't hear me incorrectly. That's what I
said. The message is for Larry and it's from me, Hank,
and it is just as I said: *I . . . love . . . you.* Thanks.
   [*Hangs up*]

MICHAEL
Seven points total! Hank, you're ahead, baby. You're
way, way ahead of everybody!

ALAN
Why? . . . Oh, Hank, why? Why did you do that?

HANK
Because I do love him. And I don't care who knows it.

ALAN
Don't say that.

HANK
Why not? It's the truth.

ALAN
I can't believe you.

HANK
    [*Directly to* ALAN]
I left my wife and family for Larry.

ALAN
I'm really not interested in hearing about it.

MICHAEL
Sure you are. Go ahead, Hankola, tell him all about it.

ALAN
No! I don't want to hear it. It's disgusting!
    [*A beat*]

HANK
Some men do it for another woman.

ALAN
Well, I could understand *that*. That's *normal*.

HANK
It just doesn't always work out that way, Alan. No matter how you might want it to. And God knows, nobody ever wanted it more than I did. I really and truly felt that I was in love with my wife when I married her. It wasn't altogether my trying to prove something to myself. I did love her and she loved me. But . . . there was always that something there . . .

DONALD
You mean your attraction to your own sex.

HANK
Yes.

ALAN
Always?

HANK
I don't know. I suppose so.

EMORY
I've known what I was since I was four years old.

MICHAEL
Everybody's always known it about *you*, Emory.

DONALD
I've always known it about myself too.

HANK
I don't know when it was that I started admitting it to myself. For so long I either labeled it something else or denied it completely.

MICHAEL
Christ-was-I-drunk-last-night.

HANK
And then there came a time when I just couldn't lie to myself any more . . . I thought about it but I never did anything about it. I think the first time was during my wife's last pregnancy. We lived near New Haven—in the country. She and the kids still live there. Well, anyway, there was a teachers' meeting here in New York. She didn't feel up to the trip and I came alone. And that day on the train I began to think about it and think about it and think about it. I thought of nothing else the whole trip. And within fifteen minutes after I had arrived I had picked up a guy in the men's room of Grand Central Station.

ALAN
  [*Quietly*]
Jesus.

HANK

I'd never done anything like that in my life before and I was scared to death. But he turned out to be a nice fellow. I've never seen him again and it's funny I can't even remember his name any more.

[*A beat*]

Anyway. After that, it got easier.

HAROLD

Practice makes perfect.

HANK

And then . . . sometime later . . . not very long after, Larry was in New Haven and we met at a party my wife and I had gone in town for.

EMORY

And your real troubles began.

HANK

That was two years ago.

LARRY

Why am I always the goddamn villain in the piece! If I'm not thought of as a happy-home wrecker, I'm an impossible son of a bitch to live with!

HAROLD

Guilt turns to hostility. Isn't that right, Michael?

MICHAEL

Go stick your tweezers in your cheek.

LARRY

I'm fed up to the teeth with everybody feeling so god-damn sorry for poor shat-upon Hank.

EMORY

Aw, Larry, everybody knows you're Frieda Fickle.

LARRY

I've never made any promises and I never intend to. It's my right to lead my sex life without answering to *anybody*—Hank included! And if those terms are not acceptable, then we must not live together. Numerous relations is a part of the way I am!

EMORY

You don't have to be gay to be a wanton.

LARRY

By the way I am, I don't mean being gay—I mean my sexual appetite. And I don't think of myself as a wanton. Emory, you are the most promiscuous person I know.

EMORY

I am not promiscuous at all!

MICHAEL

Not by choice. By design. Why would anybody want to go to bed with a flaming little sissy like you?

BERNARD

Michael!

MICHAEL
    [*To* EMORY]
Who'd make a pass at you—I'll tell you who—nobody. Except maybe some fugitive from the Braille Institute.

BERNARD
    [*To* EMORY]
Why do you let him talk to you that way?

HAROLD
Physical beauty is not everything.

MICHAEL
Thank you, Quasimodo.

LARRY
What do you think it's like living with the goddamn
gestapo! I can't breathe without getting the third de-
gree!

MICHAEL
Larry, it's your turn to call.

LARRY
I can't take all that let's-be-faithful-and-never-look-at-
another-person routine. It just doesn't work. If you
want to promise that, fine. Then do it and stick to it.
But if you *have* to promise it—as far as I'm concerned
—nothing finishes a relationship faster.

HAROLD
Give me Librium or give me Meth.

BERNARD
    [*Intoxicated now*]
Yeah, freedom, baby! Freedom!

LARRY
You gotta have it! It can't work any other way. And
the ones who swear their undying fidelity are lying.
Most of them, anyway—ninety percent of them. They
cheat on each other constantly and lie through their
teeth. I'm sorry, I can't be like that and it drives Hank
up the wall.

HANK
There is that ten percent.

LARRY
The only way it stands a chance is with some sort of an understanding.

HANK
I've tried to go along with that.

LARRY
Aw, *come on!*

HANK
I agreed to an agreement.

LARRY
Your agreement.

MICHAEL
What agreement?

LARRY
A ménage.

HAROLD
The lover's agreement.

LARRY
Look, I know a lot of people think it's the answer. They don't consider it cheating. But it's not my style.

HANK
Well, *I* certainly didn't want it.

LARRY
Then who suggested it?

HANK
It was a compromise.

LARRY
Exactly.

HANK
And you agreed.

LARRY
I didn't agree to anything. You agreed to your own proposal and *informed me* that I agreed.

COWBOY
I don't understand. What's a me . . . menaa . . .

MICHAEL
A ménage à trois, baby. Two's company—three's a ménage.

COWBOY
Oh.

HANK
It works for some.

LARRY
Well, I'm not one for group therapy. I'm sorry, I can't relate to anyone or anything that way. I'm old-fashioned—I like 'em all, but I like 'em one at a time!

MICHAEL
[*To* LARRY]
Did you like Donald as a single side attraction?
[*Pause*]

LARRY
Yes. I did.

DONALD
So did I, Larry.

LARRY
[*To* DONALD, *referring to* MICHAEL]
Did you tell him?

DONALD
No.

MICHAEL
It was perfectly obvious from the moment you walked in. What was that song and dance about having seen each other but never having met?

DONALD
It was true. We saw each other in the baths and went to bed together but we never spoke a word and never knew each other's name.

EMORY
You had better luck than I do. If I don't get arrested, my trick announces upon departure that he's been exposed to hepatitis!

MICHAEL
In spring a young man's fancy turns to a fancy young man.

LARRY
[*To* HANK]
Don't look at me like that. You've been playing footsie with the Blue Book all night.

DONALD
I think he only wanted to show you what's good for the gander is good for the gander.

HANK
That's right.

LARRY

[*To* HANK]

I suppose you'd like the three of us to have a go at it.

HANK

At least it'd be together.

LARRY

That point eludes me.

HANK

What kind of an understanding do you *want!*

LARRY

Respect—for each other's freedom. With no need to lie or pretend. In my own way, Hank, I love you, but you have to understand that even though I do want to go on living with you, sometimes there may be others. I don't want to flaunt it in your face. If it happens, I know I'll never mention it. But if you ask me, I'll tell you. I don't want to hurt you but I won't lie to you if you want to know anything about me.

BERNARD

He gets points.

MICHAEL

What?

BERNARD

He said it. He said "I love you" to Hank. He gets the bonus.

MICHAEL

He didn't call him.

DONALD

He called him. He just didn't use the telephone.

MICHAEL
Then he doesn't get any points.

BERNARD
He gets five points!

MICHAEL
He didn't use the telephone. He doesn't get a goddamn thing!
[LARRY *goes to the phone, picks up the receiver, looks at the number of the second line, dials. A beat. The phone rings*]

LARRY
It's for you, Hank. Why don't you take it upstairs?
[*The phone continues to ring.* HANK *gets up, goes up the stairs to the bedroom. Pause. He presses the second-line button, picks up the receiver. Everyone downstairs is silent*]

HANK
Hello?

BERNARD
One point.

LARRY
Hello, Hank.

BERNARD
Two points.

LARRY
. . . This is Larry.

BERNARD
Two more points!

LARRY
... For what it's worth, I love you.

BERNARD
Five points bonus!

HANK
I'll ... I'll try.

LARRY
I will too.
    [*Hangs up.* HANK *hangs up*]

BERNARD
That's ten points total!

EMORY
Larry's the winner!

HAROLD
Well, that wasn't as much fun as I thought it would be.

MICHAEL
THE GAME ISN'T OVER YET!
    [HANK *moves toward the bed into darkness*]
Your turn, Alan.
    [MICHAEL *gets the phone, slams it down in front of*
    ALAN]
PICK UP THE PHONE, BUSTER!

EMORY
Michael, don't!

MICHAEL
STAY OUT OF THIS!

EMORY
You don't have to, Alan. You don't have to.

ALAN
Emory . . . I'm sorry for what I did before.
[*A beat*]

EMORY
. . . Oh, forget it.

MICHAEL
Forgive us our trespasses. Christ, now you're both
joined at the goddamn hip! You can decorate his home,
Emory—
—and he can get you out of jail the next time you're
arrested on a morals charge.
[*A beat*]
Who are you going to call, Alan?
[*No response*]
Can't remember anyone? Well, maybe you need a min-
ute to think. Is that it?
[*No response*]

HAROLD
I believe this will be the final round.

COWBOY
Michael, aren't you going to call anyone?

HAROLD
How could he? He's never loved anyone.

MICHAEL
[*Sings the classic vaudeville walk-off to* HAROLD]
"No matter how you figger,
 It's tough to be a nigger,
  [*Indicates* BERNARD]
 But it's tougher
 To be a Jeeeew-ooouu-oo!"

[167]

DONALD

My God, Michael, you're a charming host.

HAROLD

Michael doesn't have charm, Donald. Michael has countercharm.

[LARRY *crosses to the stairs*]

MICHAEL

Going somewhere?

[LARRY *stops, turns to* MICHAEL]

LARRY

Yes. Excuse me.

[*Turns, goes up the stairs*]

MICHAEL

You're going to miss the end of the game.

LARRY

[*Pauses on stairs*]

You can tell me how it comes out.

MICHAEL

I never reveal an ending. And no one will be reseated during the climactic revelation.

LARRY

With any luck, I won't be back until it's all over.

[*Turns, continues up the stairs into the dark*]

MICHAEL

[*Into* ALAN's *ear*]

What do you suppose is going on up there? Hmmm, Alan? What do you imagine Larry and Hank are doing? Hmmmmm? Shooting marbles?

[168]

EMORY

Whatever they're doing, they're not hurting anyone.

HAROLD

And they're minding their own business.

MICHAEL

And you mind yours, Harold. I'm warning you!
[*A beat*]

HAROLD
[*Coolly*]

Are you now? Are you warning *me*? *Me*? I'm Harold.
I'm the one person you don't warn, Michael. Because
you and I are a match. And we tread very softly with
each other because we both play each other's game too
well. Oh, I know this game you're playing. I know it
very well. And I *play* it very well. You play it very well
too. But you know what, I'm the only one that's better
at it than you are. I can beat you at it. So don't push
me. I'm warning *you*.
[*A beat.* MICHAEL *starts to laugh*]

MICHAEL

You're funny, Hallie. A laff riot. Isn't he funny, Alan?
Or, as you might say, isn't he amusing. He's an amusing faggot, isn't he? Or, as you might say, freak. That's
what you called Emory, wasn't it? A freak? A pansy?
My, what an antiquated vocabulary you have. I'm surprised you didn't say sodomite or pederast.
[*A beat*]
You'd better let me bring you up to date. Now it's not
so new, but it might be new to you—
[*A beat*]
Have you heard the term "closet queen"? Do you know
what that means? Do you know what it means to be
"in the closet"?

EMORY

Don't, Michael. It won't help anything to explain what it means.

MICHAEL

He already knows. He knows very, very well what a closet queen is. Don't you, Alan?
[*Pause*]

ALAN

Michael, if you are insinuating that I am homosexual, I can only say that you are mistaken.

MICHAEL

Am I?
[*A beat*]
What about Justin Stuart?

ALAN

... What about ... Justin Stuart?

MICHAEL

You were in love with him, that's what about him.
[*A beat*]
And *that* is who you are going to call.

ALAN

Justin and I were very good friends. That is all. Unfortunately, we had a parting of the ways and that was the end of the friendship. We have not spoken for years. I most certainly will not call him now.

MICHAEL

According to Justin, the friendship was quite passionate.

ALAN

What do you mean?

MICHAEL

I mean that you slept with him in college. Several times.

ALAN

That is not true!

MICHAEL

Several times. One time, it's youth. Twice, a phase maybe. Several times, *you like it!*

ALAN

IT'S NOT TRUE!

MICHAEL

Yes, it is. Because Justin Stuart *is* homosexual. He comes to New York on occasion. He calls me. I've taken him to parties. Larry "had" him once. *I* have slept with Justin Stuart. And he has told me all about *you.*

ALAN

Then he told you a lie.
   [*A beat*]

MICHAEL

You were obsessed with Justin. That's all you talked about, morning, noon, and night. You started doing it about Hank upstairs tonight. What an attractive fellow he is and all that transparent crap.

ALAN

He *is* an attractive fellow. What's wrong with saying so?

MICHAEL

Would you like to join him and Larry right now?

ALAN

I said he was attractive. That's all.

MICHAEL

How many times do you have to say it? How many
times did you have to say it about Justin: what a good
tennis player he was; what a good dancer he was; what
a good body he had; what good taste he had; how
bright he was—how *amusing* he was—how the girls
were all mad for him—what close friends you were.

ALAN

We . . . we . . . were . . . very close . . . very good . . .
friends. *That's all!*

MICHAEL

It was *obvious*—and when you did it around Fran it
was downright embarrassing. Even she must have had
her doubts about you.

ALAN

Justin . . . lied. If he told you that, he lied. It is a lie. A
vicious lie. He'd say anything about me now to get
even. He could never get over the fact that *I* dropped
him. But I had to. I had to because . . . he told me . . .
he told me about himself . . . he told me that he wanted
to be my lover. And I . . . I . . . told him . . . he made me
sick . . . I told him I pitied him.
    [*A beat*]

MICHAEL

You ended the friendship, Alan, because you couldn't
face the truth about yourself. You could go along,
sleeping with Justin, as long as he lied to himself and
you lied to yourself and you both dated girls and labeled yourselves men and called yourselves just fond
friends. But Justin finally had to be honest about the
truth, and you couldn't take it. You couldn't take it and
so you destroyed the friendship and your friend along
with it.

    [MICHAEL *goes to the desk and gets address book*]

[172]

ALAN
No!

MICHAEL
Justin could never understand what he'd done wrong
to make you cut him off. He blamed himself.

ALAN
No!

MICHAEL
He did until he eventually found out who he was and
what he was.

ALAN
No!

MICHAEL
But to this day he still remembers the treatment—the
scars he got from you.
[*Puts address book in front of* ALAN *on coffee
table*]

ALAN
NO!

MICHAEL
Pick up this phone and call Justin. Call him and apologize and tell him what you should have told him twelve
years ago.
[*Picks up the phone, shoves it at* ALAN]

ALAN
NO! HE LIED! NOT A WORD IS TRUE!

MICHAEL
CALL HIM!
[ALAN *won't take the phone*]

All right then, *I'll dial!*

HAROLD
You're so helpful.
[MICHAEL *starts to dial*]

ALAN
Give it to me.
[MICHAEL *hands* ALAN *the receiver.* ALAN *takes it,
hangs up for a moment, lifts it again, starts to dial.
Everyone watches silently.* ALAN *finishes dialing,
lifts the receiver to his ear*]
... Hello?

MICHAEL
One point.

ALAN
... It's ... it's Alan.

MICHAEL
Two points.

ALAN
... Yes, yes, it's *me*.

MICHAEL
Is it Justin?

ALAN
... You sound surprised.

MICHAEL
I should hope to think so—after twelve years! Two more
points.

ALAN
I ... I'm in New York. Yes. I ... won't explain now ...

I . . . I just called to tell you . . .

MICHAEL

THAT I LOVE YOU, GODDAMNIT! I LOVE YOU!

ALAN

I love you.

MICHAEL

You get the goddamn bonus. TEN POINTS TOTAL!
JACKPOT!

ALAN

I love you and I beg you to forgive me.

MICHAEL

Give me that!
  [*Snatches the phone from* ALAN]
Justin! Did you hear what that son of a bitch said!
  [*A beat.* MICHAEL *is speechless for a moment*]
. . . Fran?
  [*A beat*]
Well, of course I expected it to be you! . . .
  [*A beat*]
How are you? Me, too. Yes, yes . . . he told me every-
thing. Oh, don't thank *me*. Please . . . Please . . .
  [*A beat*]
I'll . . . I'll put him back on.
  [*A beat*]
My love to the kids . . .

ALAN

. . . Darling? I'll take the first plane I can get. Yes. I'm
sorry too. I love you very much.
  [*Hangs up, stands, crosses to the door, stops. Turns
  around, surveys the group*]
Thank you, Michael.
  [*Opens the door and exits.*

[175]

Silence. MICHAEL *slowly sinks down on the couch, covering his face.*
Pause]

COWBOY
Who won?

DONALD
It was a tie.
[HAROLD *crosses to* MICHAEL]

HAROLD
[*Calmly, coldly, clinically*]
Now it is my turn. And ready or not, Michael, here goes.
[*A beat*]
You are a sad and pathetic man. You're a homosexual and you don't want to be. But there is nothing you can do to change it. Not all your prayers to your God, not all the analysis you can buy in all the years you've got left to live. You may very well one day be able to know a heterosexual life if you want it desperately enough— if you pursue it with the fervor with which you annihilate—but you will always be homosexual as well. Always, Michael. Always. Until the day you die.
[*Turns, gathers his gifts, goes to* EMORY. EMORY *stands up unsteadily*]
Oh, friends, thanks for the nifty party and the super gift.
[*Looks toward* COWBOY]
It's just what I needed.
[EMORY *smiles.* HAROLD *gives him a hug, spots* BERNARD *sitting on the floor, head bowed*]
... Bernard, thank you.
[*No response. To* EMORY]
Will you get him home?

EMORY

Don't worry about her. I'll take care of everything.

[HAROLD *turns to* DONALD, *who is at the bar making himself another drink*]

HAROLD

Donald, good to see you.

DONALD

Good night, Harold. See you again sometime.

HAROLD

Yeah. How about a year from Shavuoth?

[HAROLD *goes to* COWBOY]

Come on, Tex. Let's go to my place.

[COWBOY *gets up, comes to him*]

Are you good in bed?

COWBOY

Well . . . I'm not like the average hustler you'd meet. I try to show a little affection—it keeps me from feeling like such a whore.

[*A beat.* HAROLD *turns.* COWBOY *opens the door for them. They start out.* HAROLD *pauses*]

HAROLD

Oh, Michael . . . thanks for the laughs. Call you to-morrow.

[*No response. A beat.* HAROLD *and* COWBOY *exit*]

EMORY

Come on, Bernard. Time to go home.

[EMORY, *frail as he is, manages to pull* BERNARD's *arm around his neck, gets him on his feet*]

Oh, Mary, you're a heavy mother.

BERNARD

[*Practically inaudible mumble*]

[177]

Why did I call? Why?

EMORY
Thank you, Michael. Good night, Donald.

DONALD
Goodbye, Emory.

BERNARD
Why . . .

EMORY
It's all right, Bernard. Everything's all right. I'm going to make you some coffee and everything's going to be all right.
[EMORY *virtually carries* BERNARD *out.* DONALD *closes the door. Silence.*
MICHAEL *slowly slips from the couch onto the floor. A beat. Then slowly he begins a low moan that increases in volume—almost like a siren. Suddenly he slams his open hands to his ears*]

MICHAEL
[*In desperate panic*]
Donald! Donald! DONALD! DONALD!
[DONALD *puts down his drink, rushes to* MICHAEL. MICHAEL *is now white with fear and tears are bursting from his eyes. He begins to gasp his words*]
Oh, no! No! What have I done! Oh, my God, what have I done!
[MICHAEL *writhing.* DONALD *holds him, cradles him in his arms*]

DONALD
Michael! Michael!

[178]

MICHAEL
[*Weeping*]
Oh, no! NO! It's beginning! The liquor is starting to
wear off and the anxiety is beginning! Oh, NO! No! I
feel it! I know it's going to happen. Donald!! Donald!
Don't leave me! Please! Please! Oh, my God, what have
I done! Oh Jesus, the guilt! I can't handle it any more.
I won't make it!

DONALD
[*Physically subduing him*]
Michael! Michael! Stop it! Stop it! I'll give you a Val-
ium—I've got some in my pocket!

MICHAEL
[*Hysterical*]
No! No! Pills and alcohol—I'll die!

DONALD
I'm not going to give you the whole bottle! Come on,
let go of me!

MICHAEL
[*Clutching him*]
NO!

DONALD
Let go of me long enough for me to get my hand in my
pocket!

MICHAEL
Don't leave!
[MICHAEL *quiets down a bit, lets go of* DONALD
*enough for him to take a small plastic bottle from
his pocket and open it to give* MICHAEL *a tran-
quilizer*]

DONALD
Here.

MICHAEL
[*Sobbing*]
I don't have any water to swallow it with!

DONALD
Well, if you'll wait one goddamn minute, I'll get you
some!
[MICHAEL *lets go of him. He goes to the bar, gets a*
glass of water and returns]
Your water, your Majesty.
[*A beat*]
Michael, stop that goddamn crying and take this pill!
[MICHAEL *straightens up, puts the pill into his*
mouth amid choking sobs, takes the water, drinks,
returns the glass to DONALD]

MICHAEL
I'm like Ole Man River—tired of livin' and scared o'
dyin'.
[DONALD *puts the glass on the bar, comes back to*
the couch, sits down. MICHAEL *collapses into his*
arms, sobbing. Pause]

DONALD
Shhhhh. Shhhhhh. Michael. Shhhhhh. Michael. Mi-
chael.
[DONALD *rocks him back and forth. He quiets.*
Pause]

MICHAEL
. . . If we . . . if we could just . . . not hate ourselves so
much. That's it, you know. If we could just *learn* not to
hate ourselves quite so very much.

DONALD
Yes, I know. I know.

[*A beat*]
Inconceivable as it may be, you used to be worse than
you are now.
[*A beat*]
Maybe with a lot more work you can help yourself
some more—if you try.

> [MICHAEL *straightens up, dries his eyes on his
> sleeve*]

MICHAEL
Who was it that used to always say, "You show me a
happy homosexual, and I'll show you a gay corpse."

DONALD
I don't know. Who was it who always used to say that?

MICHAEL
And how dare you come on with that holier-than-thou
attitude with me! "A lot more work," "if I try," indeed!
You've got a long row to hoe before you're perfect, you
know.

DONALD
I never said I didn't.

MICHAEL
And while we're on the subject—I think your analyst is
a quack.

> [MICHAEL *is sniffling.* DONALD *hands him a hand-
> kerchief. He takes it and blows his nose*]

DONALD
Earlier you said he was a prick.

MICHAEL
That's right. He's a prick quack. Or a quack prick,
whichever you prefer.

> [DONALD *gets up from the couch, goes for his drink*]

[181]

DONALD

[*Heaving a sigh*]
Harold was right. You'll never change.

MICHAEL

Come back, Donald. Come back, Shane.

DONALD

I'll come back when you have another anxiety attack.

MICHAEL

I need you. Just like Mickey Mouse needs Minnie Mouse—just like Donald Duck needs Minnie Duck. Mickey needs Donnie.

DONALD

My name is Donald. I am called Donald. You must never call anyone called Donald Donnie . . .

MICHAEL

[*Grabs his head, moans*]
Ohhhhh . . . icks! Icks! Terrible icks! Tomorrow is going to be an ick-packed day. It's going to be a Bad Day at Black Rock. A day of nerves, nerves, and more nerves!

[MICHAEL *gets up from the couch, surveys the wreckage of the dishes and gift wrappings*]
Do you suppose there's any possibility of just burning this room?

[*A beat*]

DONALD

Why do you think he stayed, Michael? Why do you think he took all of that from you?

MICHAEL

There are no accidents. He was begging to get killed. He was dying for somebody to let him have it and he got what he wanted.

DONALD

He could have been telling the truth—Justin could have lied.

MICHAEL

Who knows? What time is it?

DONALD

It seems like it's day after tomorrow.
     [MICHAEL *goes to the kitchen door, pokes his head
     in. Comes back into the room carrying a raincoat*]

MICHAEL

It's early.
     [*Goes to a closet door, takes out a blazer, puts it
     on*]

DONALD

What does life *hold*? Where're you going?

MICHAEL

The bedroom is ocupado and I don't want to go to sleep anyway until I try to walk off the booze. If I went to sleep like this, when I wake up they'd have to put me in a padded cell—not that that's where I don't belong.
     [*A beat*]
And ... and ... there's a midnight mass at St. Malachy's that all the show people go to. I think I'll walk over there and catch it.

DONALD

     [*Raises his glass*]
Well, pray for me.

MICHAEL

     [*Indicates bedroom*]
Maybe they'll be gone by the time I get back.

DONALD

Well, *I* will be—just as soon as I knock off that bottle of brandy.

MICHAEL

Will I see you next Saturday?

DONALD

Unless you have other plans.

MICHAEL

No.
[*Turns to go*]

DONALD

Michael?

MICHAEL

[*Stops, turns back*]
What?

DONALD

Did he ever tell you why he was crying on the phone —what it was he *had* to tell you?

MICHAEL

No. It must have been that he'd left Fran. Or maybe it was something else and he changed his mind.

DONALD

Maybe so.
[*A beat*]
I wonder why he left her.
[*A pause*]

MICHAEL

. . . As my father said to me when he died in my arms, "I don't understand any of it. I never did."

[*A beat.* DONALD *goes to his stack of books, selects one, and sits in a chair*]

Turn out the lights when you leave, will you?
　　[DONALD *nods.* MICHAEL *looks at him for a long silent moment.* DONALD *turns his attention to his book, starts to read.* MICHAEL *opens the door and exits*]

Curtain

An astonishing new book
by a dazzling young writer

Stop-Time

by Frank Conroy

Frank Conroy is a sensitive young writer who has written a new kind of book for a new kind of world. STOP-TIME is a distinguished and unique autobiography with the intimate unprotected candor of a novel. It is the story of growing up in an America of autos, cities, broken families, sexual anarchy and rootless discontent. It is one of the extraordinary books of our decade.

"A documentary of chilling perception, a book whose honesty and evocation of youth is a triumph. STOP-TIME, free of rancor, rich with the half-mad, lonely characters who people our times, is one of the finest books about growing up I have ever read"
—*New York Times Book Review*

"Intensely readable . . . no one who starts it will fail to finish it . . . unquestionably a significant work of contemporary art . . . an important new American writer"

—*Commonweal*

A DELL BOOK 95c

A forthcoming major motion picture

How many of these Dell bestsellers have you read?

The Naked Ape by Desmond Morris   95c

Nicholas and Alexandra by Robert K. Massie $1.25

The Tower of Babel by Morris L. West $1.25

Pretty Maids All In A Row by Francis Pollini   95c

Jefferson Square by Noel Gerson   95c

The Brand Name Calorie Counter by Corinne T. Netzer $1.25

The Survivors by Anne Edwards   95c

The Doctor's Quick Weight-Loss Diet
by I. Maxwell Stillman and S. Sinclair Baker   95c

Stop-Time by Frank Conroy   95c

The Deal by G. William Marshall   95c

The Gospel Singer by Harry Crews   95c

Horse Under Water (A Putnam Book) by Len Deighton   75c

Three Into Two Won't Go by Andrea Newman   95c

The Ginger Man by J. P. Donleavy   95c

The Monkey Puzzle Tree by Nona Coxhead   95c

The Operating Theater by Vincent Brome   95c

Soul On Ice (A Delta Edition) by Eldridge Cleaver $1.95

If you cannot obtain copies of these titles at your local bookseller, just send the price (plus 10c per copy for handling and postage) to Dell Books, Box 2291, Grand Central Post Office, New York, N.Y. 10017. No postage or handling charge is required on any order of five or more books.

MIDNIGHT COWBOY

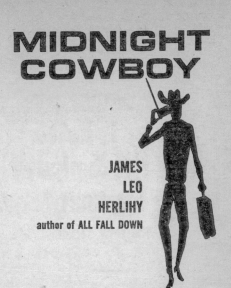

JAMES
LEO
HERLIHY
author of ALL FALL DOWN

"This is the story of Joe Buck, a loner. Joe has never known how to reach out and make contact with another human being. His only clue to communication lies in his body. Dressed up in a new cowboy outfit, he heads for New York City, where rich women will pay to possess him. MIDNIGHT COWBOY is concerned with the descent of Joe Buck into New York's nighttime dregs and of his break-through to feeling for someone outside of himself. . . ."
—*New York Herald Tribune*

"Brilliant . . . dazzling talent"
—*Newsweek*

Don't miss the great United Artists motion picture starring
Dustin Hoffman and Jon Voight.

DELL 75c

2⁵⁰

A NEW KIND OF PLAY
TAKES CENTER STAGE

"One of the most controversial plays of recent years . . . a breakthrough . . . The 'boys' in Mart Crowley's band are human beings."

REX REED
The New York Times

"An area which stage realism has not yet explored . . . But now along comes a view of it that is knowing rather than sensationalistic, sympathetic rather than apologetic or defiant, and, above all, unruffled . . . an original achievement."

JOHN SIMON
The New York Magazine

AG

"All the once forbidden words are there, and the action is highly explicit, but the play by Mart Crowley doesn't strike me as a mere exercise in sensationalism. It has its share of outspoken humor but . . . don't mistake THE BOYS IN THE BAND for a cheap and tawdry play."

RICHARD WATTS, JR.
New York Post

(Please turn page)

AND THE WORD IS OUT

"The frankest and funniest homosexual play ever put on a stage . . . Though banter ricochets off the apartment's walls all evening, Mr. Crowley is aiming at something much more serious. Each mordant thrust is aimed to hurt not the audience but the characters, searing off one more layer from the protective coating each of Mr. Crowley's gay men has built around himself."

The National Observer

"Neither obscene nor disgusting . . . a drama with honesty and insight . . . valid and vivid . . . an engrossing narrative . . . extremely sensitive in its revelations . . . THE BOYS IN THE BAND is a success because it is a good play. It works. It comes alive. It shows us people."

Chicago Daily News